MARLOW
A Pictorial History

Aerial view of Marlow, *c.*1968.

To Audrey.

MARLOW
A Pictorial History

Rachel Brown
&
Julian Hunt

Rachel Brown.

Julian Hunt

Phillimore

1994

Published by
Phillimore & Co. Ltd.
Shopwyke Manor Barn, Chichester, West Sussex
in association with
Buckinghamshire County Library

ISBN 0 85033 942 1

Printed and bound in Great Britain by
BIDDLES LTD.
Guildford, Surrey

List of Illustrations

Frontispiece: Aerial view of Marlow, *c*.1968

Acknowledgements

This book is the result of happy co-operation between Buckinghamshire County Library and the Marlow Society, drawing on the resources of the local collections at the libraries in Marlow and Aylesbury and the Society's archive of Marlow's past. Particular thanks are due to Bill Purser of the Marlow Society who has generously made available the results of her extensive research on the town, to Joan Rogers, who drew the fine maps used in the introduction, and to John Anderson, who loaned a copy of the rules of the open fields.

The photographs used in this book are not only chosen because they show Marlow in an attractive light but also because they illustrate aspects of the town's history which the authors wish to emphasise. Most of the photographs are from the County Reference Library in Aylesbury, or from Marlow Library. Where suitable illustrations were not available, new phtographs were taken by Brian Drage of the Marlow Society. These are numbered 4-5, 7-9, 55, 57, 70, 72-5, 106-109, 112, 115-16, 119-20 and 138. Other photographs from the collection of the Marlow Society are numbered 14, 59, 62, 76, 80, 89-90, 101, 103, 110-111, 131, 135, 139-41, 143 and 154. Many of these were copied, with great skill and patience, by Brian Drage from originals loaned to the Marlow Society.

Buckinghamshire County Museum supplied the photographs numbered 17, 23, 37, 40-1, 79 and 91. Buckinghamshire County Record Office supplied a copy of the Turnpike Act numbered 52. The Royal Commission on Historic Monuments (RCHM) supplied the photographs numbered 6, 15, 38-9, 63, 66, 68, 84, 130, 132-4 and 136-7. The National Museum of Wales gave permission to reproduce the portrait of Thomas Williams (96) and Messrs Whitbread contributed the photographs of the brewery numbered 44-46. Sir William Borlase's School gave permission to reproduce the plan of Marlow Mills (29), Messrs. Simmons & Lawrence contributed items 81 and 124-5, and the Committee of Management of Marlow Regatta agreed to the reproduction of item 152. Mr. J.H. Venn of Great Missenden supplied prints from the negatives of the late Stanley Freese. These are numbered 12 and 34 whilst number 60 is from Mr. Venn's own collection.

Individual contributors were Mrs. Mary Adams (77), Fred Boxall (18), Jock Cairns (100), Robert Clark (61 and 126), John Fontannaz (24), Mrs. Harvey (113), Mrs. Hillier (3), Alan Holmes (31, 35, 42 and 85), Peter Kingsford (88), Mr. and Mrs. David Lovell (117-8), Malcolm McIntyre-Ure (Frontispiece and 22), Alan Morris (10), Mrs. Grace Price (47), Mrs. Reeves (114 and 127), Margaret Smith (58 and 67), and David Wilson (36).

Introduction

In 1871, a 25-ft. dug-out canoe, thought to date from the Iron Age, was raised from the Thames at Bourne End. Here was proof, if proof were needed, that the Thames was a thoroughfare in prehistoric times. There must have been many suitable embarkation points and we can only speculate on the age of Marlow as a trading post on the river.

There are traces of Roman settlements in and around Marlow, including what was perhaps a Roman cloth factory out towards Medmenham. A minor Roman road is claimed to cross the Marlow to Lane End road and there may have been a Roman villa near the site of what used to be Marlow cattle market, near the old railway station. Local historian Francis Colmer suggested that a minor Roman highway ran through Marlow from east to west, with a right-angled spur to the river—perhaps the beginning of the T-shaped town centre of today.

The Saxons knew the place as Merelaue (land remaining after a lake is drained). The fact that Marlow had a topographical name does not presuppose a late settlement date, for many Saxon place names are now thought to describe suitability for habitation. During the the Saxon period, the manor of Marlow must have prospered, for Domesday Book finds 107 taxable individuals and assesses the four estates there at 35 hides—a higher taxation than the four Wycombe manors and an unusually large figure for Buckinghamshire. A hide was a Saxon measurement of land area—probably for taxation purposes—supposed to be sufficient to support one family for one year. It therefore varied with the district but here it was about 120 acres.

Marlow was part of the hundred of Desborough whose meeting place was Desborough Castle, a hill-fort in West Wycombe. The hundred may have originated as a tax gathering unit of 100 hides, but hundreds developed their own courts dealing with administrative matters beyond the scope of the manor court. The multiple of ten is seen within the manor, where heads of household were placed in tythings—ten men who stood surety for one another's good behaviour. There is a record of a shepherd from Harleyford who committed a murder and then fled. The justices of Dunstable in 1227 fined the remaining nine men in his tything. Parishes were grouped in hundreds down the centuries until 1894 when District Councils were established.

In medieval times Marlow must have been a town of some size and importance. The hundred rolls (Rotuli Hundredorum) of 1278-9 names almost two hundred Marlow burgesses (citizens with municipal rights). It is interesting that many had names derived from their calling, such as Rob Piscator (Robert the fisherman), Ric le Flesmongere (Richard the butcher) and Wills le Carpent (William the carpenter). The figure of two hundred burgesses implies a town of 1,000 people or more—a considerable population for the period. This compares with a Domesday population of about 500, showing that Marlow had expanded in line with population growth over the whole country in the medieval period. The founding of the chantry of St Mary would be for charitable or civic purposes, possibly connected with the need to maintain the bridge. A priest was probaby employed to say masses for the souls of burgesses, both living and dead, and the name Chapel Street probably dates from this period. Another medieval town institution was the short-lived hospital, or travellers' rest, of St Thomas, known to have existed here in the 14th century, which gave the name to Spittal Street.

In the 14th century, there followed a series of bad harvests and plagues so that the population everywhere declined sharply. No doubt this was reflected in Marlow, for the town does not seem to have regained its early importance except perhaps for a brief period in the 17th and 18th centuries. At this time, many houses were rebuilt or 'new fronted' and there must have been sufficient money and patronage to enable local shopkeepers to hold large stocks of luxury goods. The 1688 probate inventory of Sylvester Widmore, a Marlow mercer, lists various types of cloth and a wide range of other goods in his shop and warehouses.

By the 19th century, the majority of Marlow's inhabitants were very poor. In May 1814, a letter from the National School appealing for funds from the 'National Society' stated that Marlow had about 4,000 inhabitants and that the majority were 'very necessitous'. The situation was not much better in 1847 when a certain James Thorne thought Marlow a second rate agricultural town. 'Shops are small and of a commonplace kind and the countrymen hereabouts are not of a mirthful cast. The population is very poor, the streets are mean and have a poverty stricken aspect—there are more evident signs of vice than is at all common in country towns of the same size and class.'

The Manors

Before the Norman Conquest, the largest of the four Marlow estates had been held by the Saxon Earl Algar but he was dispossessed, and his lands were bestowed on Queen Matilda, wife of the Conqueror. Domesday Book records a large population, comprising 35 tenant farmers, 25 smallholders and one serf, whose families might together number over three hundred. Despite the fact that there were as many as 26 ploughs at work, the estate is taxed at a modest 15 hides. There was a mill with the comparatively high valuation of 20s., woodland for 1,000 hogs and a fishery producing 1,000 eels (eels were obviously plentiful in the river then and they remained so for many centuries).

After the Conquest, Great Marlow manor was part of the Queen's honour of Gloucester and was inherited or bestowed as such—belonging in 1107 to Robert Fitzroy, an illegitimate son of Henry I, and in 1290 to Gilbert de Clare, husband of Edward I's daughter Joan. Later (1316) the manor was held by Hugh le Despenser, Earl of Gloucester, who was hanged in 1326. His lands continued to his heirs through his widow, but in 1400 a Thomas le Despenser was beheaded. Joan, Queen of Henry IV, received custody of the manor during the minority of Thomas's son. In the 15th century the Earls of Warwick held Marlow but long leases were granted and the freehold was eventually conveyed to the Paget family, through which it descended for several generations. In 1669, it passed through purchase to a local family named Moore, one of whom, Robert Moore, presented a brass bushel measure to Marlow's market house. Moore died in 1681 and the probate inventory of his goods shows him to be a man of substance with valuable plate, pewter and brass, and several feather beds in his house at Marlow. He had considerable 'outside' goods, including those in a brewhouse and 'one hundred and forty load of billet lying at the wharf' (presumably ready for shipment down river).

The manor of Great Marlow was purchased in 1735 by Sir William Clayton, nephew of the banker Robert Clayton, who had been Lord Mayor of London in 1679. By this time the Clayton estate included other sub-manors which had quite separate histories.

Harleyford

Harleyford Manor began as an estate (of one hide) carved out of Great Marlow Manor by one of the Earls of Gloucester for a subtenant in 1183. By 1209 the estate had passed to a William de Harleyford and descended to his heirs until the late 14th century when the family died out. It then passed through various owners including Tucker Bold who, in 1542, obtained a licence from the Bishop of Lincoln to have a priest officiate within his chapel in his house at Harleyford, because he was 'so far from the church'. In 1599, Harleyford was purchased by a Miles Hobart whose son, also named Miles, became MP for Marlow in 1627. This second Miles Hobart was killed in a coaching accident and his estate passed to two cousins—one of whom had difficulty inheriting because her father had been attainted for piracy! Lord Paget, owner of Great Marlow manor, finally bought Harleyford and resided there for almost the whole of the Civil War. The manor of Harleyford thereafter descended with the manor of Marlow.

Little Marlow

Two of the manors, named Merlaue or Berlaue in Domesday Book, can be associated with Little Marlow. The five-hide estate owned in 1086 by the Conqueror's half brother, the Bishop of Bayeux, includes a water mill and a fishery yielding 500 eels. Much of the land was later given to endow the Benedictine priory of Little Marlow. The other estate, of $8^5/8$ hides, belonged at Domesday to Miles Crispin, and was later divided between Crispin's tenants, Ralf and Roger, the latter's portion now being represented by Westhorpe House, Little Marlow.

Widmere

The fourth entry for Marlow in Domesday Book describes a $6^3/8$ hide estate held by Walter Vernon. This seems an odd valuation, but, if the $8^5/8$ estate of Miles Crispin in Little Marlow is added, it is apparent that the two were once assessed together at 15 hides. Vernon's estate has been linked with the land in Marlow granted at an early date to several religious orders. In 1248, the Master of St Thomas' Hospital, Southwark, sold property in Marlow to the Knights Hospitallers (or Knights of St John of Jerusalem), a miltary order founded at the time of the first crusade. In 1268 these lands included 'a messuage in Wodmere'. Another military order, the Knights Templars (founded in Jerusalem by the crusaders), had land in Marlow as well as their settlement at Bisham. It has been conjectured that the Knights Templars built the first Marlow Bridge in order to link their two estates. The Knights Templars fell into disrepute and the order was dissolved in 1312. Their land in Marlow appears to have been added to that of the rival order, the Knights Hospitallers. It may have been the Knights Hospitallers who built the chapel which survives at Widmere, but in 1338, their estate, confusingly described as having 'formerly belonged to the Templars', was let to a tenant and there were no knights there. The crypt of Widmere Chapel is probably the oldest surviving structure in the parish of Great Marlow.

After the dissolution of all monastic orders under Henry VIII, Widmere was sold to the Russells of Chenies, who in turn, in 1623, sold it to Sir William Borlase, lord of the manor of Little Marlow. There is a record of John Borlase, MP for Marlow, holding a court there in 1671. The property passed through the heirs of a daughter of Sir William Borlase to the Temples of Stowe and finally descended to the Claytons of Harleyford. Thomas Langley records that a sale in 1747 was postponed while Richard Temple transplanted a quantity of beech from Widmere woods to the grounds of Stowe. By the time Langley wrote (1790s) 'they were of great size and much admired'. Thus by the 18th century, three of Marlow's manors were in the hands of the Clayton family, whose estate was not finally broken up until after the First World War.

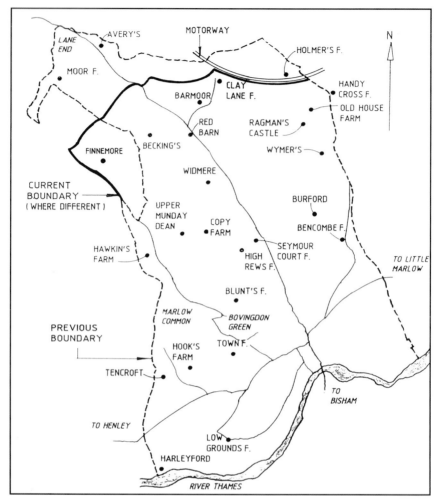

A map of Great Marlow parish showing the positions of the old farmsteads. The old boundary is marked with a dotted line and the modern changes with a bold black line.

Seymour Court

Two more ancient estates originate from early grants to religious houses. One such is Seymour Court, belonging to Muchelney Abbey in Somerset. At the dissolution, it was acquired with the abbey by Edward Seymour, Earl of Hereford, but, after an exchange of lands with the crown, it was granted to the Dean and Chapter of Bristol who sold it to the local brewing family of Wethered as late as 1862. A John Semor is recorded here in 1425, but the local tradition of Seymour Court being the birthplace of Jane Seymour is very doubtful.

Barmoor

Barmer (Barmoor) was separated from the manor of Great Marlow in the early 13th century and given to St Thomas' Hospital in Southwark. The estate included three mills adjoining 'a meadow called Gosmer', which links them with the site of the corn and paper mills which survived until 1965. After the dissolution of the monasteries, the mills were let by the crown to successive tenants including John Brinkhurst, founder of Marlow's almshouses charity.

The Common Fields

Widmere, Seymours and Barmoor were upland estates with old-enclosed fields taken in from the woodland or waste as need arose. In the valley, however, the manor of Great Marlow had at least three common arable fields where the 'strip system' of farming survived into the 19th century. The three fields, named Marefield, the Upper Field and the Lower Field, were situated to the north east and south east of the town. In a given year, one field might be sown with wheat, another with peas and beans and the third left fallow. In the following year, the crops would be rotated so that the land could recover, but there was always a fallow field providing pasture for the animals of the town. The strips were small in area (often less than an acre) arranged in groups called furlongs. Each strip belonged to a different owner whose lease or deeds would define the position of the strip in a particular furlong by reference to the names of the proprietors of the two neighbouring strips. The system probably arose in Saxon times as a means of giving farmers equal holdings of differing qualities of land and the right to pasture animals on the fallow field. By the time it was introduced into Marlow it was more likely to have been the prevailing agricultural fashion. Over the centuries, by purchase and exchange, the strips were grouped and were often let to tenants, many of whom grazed cattle on the land rather than growing crops. In the 19th century, the Dean and Chapter of Bristol (owners of Barmoor Manor) and the Dean and Chapter of Gloucester (owners of the Parsonage and the right to collect the tithes) both owned strips in Marlow's open fields.

The records of the 18th-century court leets and court barons (manorial courts) for the manor of Marlow make very clear that the rules about grazing and other uses of the common fields were strictly enforced and fines were imposed on transgressors. 'No person shall depasture more than two sheep for one acre of land that he or she may occupy in the Common Fields—on pain of forfeiting to the lord 5/- for each sheep (extra) and for each offence. No person to cut grass off the baulkes (dividing strips) until the Common Fields be rid of corn. No person to put sheep on the wheat stubbles until September 26th (Hollyrood Day) or the barley stubbles until Michaelmas, (or any animals until the fields are entirely rid of corn) nor into any of the common meadows until All Hallows Day (November 1st) in each and every year and to come out of the meadows on Candlemas Day (February 2nd). No person to sow any part of the common field which ought to lie fallow.'

Enclosures were to be thrown open (those who had enclosed land were fined—including the vicar!). Public footways were to be carefully retained and it was noted that the chalkpit in Oxford Lane was a 'common pit' and Limmer pond a 'common pond' for the use of the inhabitants of Great Marlow. Straying animals were impounded and owners fined as also those who did not clean their ditches or properly fence their ponds. One man was fined for cutting down an oak tree near Red Barn, for it belonged to the lord of the manor.

The Enclosure of the Open Fields

C.S. Reed, in an 1856 report on agriculture in Buckinghamshire, vehemently condemned the open field system of Marlow. 'Anyone who wishes to see the horrors of open lands should visit Great Marlow Field.' The strip system of the common fields was ended by the Marlow Enclosure Award of 1855. Commissioners appointed by Act of Parliament valued all the strips in the open fields and reallocated the land in blocks. Some land was sold to defray the enclosure expenses, some land was exchanged, new roads and paths were laid out while others were 'stopped up', and, after all the allotments had been made, some land was entrusted to the churchwardens as places for exercise and recreation for the people of the parish. One such area was a field near Gossmore—it was always known as the 'recreation ground' and is still part of an area used as such.

The Marlow enclosure was too late to lead to the rebuilding of farmhouses and their relocation on the new allotments of land in the former common fields. Field House Farm is the only example of this process and the farm has now been built on, together with most of the former open field land.

The strips in the open fields are clearly shown on this map where the new allotments under the 1855 Enclosure Award are superimposed on the 1843 tithe map.

Tithes

Payment of tithes to the church, either in kind or in money, was a survival from the days when agriculture was the main occupation of the people. Tithes were the tenth part of the produce of the land; the great tithes, such as corn, oats and wood, were paid to the rector, and the small tithes, a tenth part of the produce of both stock and labour, such as wool, pigs and milk, went to the vicar. The system was resented by the farming community and considered an unfair burden, particularly as no such tax was levied on the products of factories. Edward Sawyer of Great Marlow made this abundantly clear in a letter of 24 July 1830:

> To the Most Reverend Father of the Church of England
> Archbishop of Canterbury ... There is many
> unpleasant things happen in taking the tithes in
> kind after the farmer have done his best for his
> crop to have the tenth taken by the Rector or the
> Layman as taking the tithes is the greatest evil in
> the country ... As I am plain John Bull knows more
> about farming than I do about Grammar ...

The tithes of the parish of Great Marlow were owned by the Dean and Chapter of Gloucester and were divided into two halves, according to local custom. In 1843, the date of the Marlow tithe award, the right to collect the tithes was leased to James Deane of Tunbridge Wells, whose subtenant, Henry Webb of High Rews Farm, took his tithes largely in kind, and Mary Wright of Marlow Mills, who took her half in money payments. The old road—now a bridleway—which leads from Munday Dean Lane up to High Rews and Widmere, marks the old line of the tithe division. The lessees were to maintain the chancel of the church and the parsonage house and to pay the vicar an income in lieu of his small tithes. The Parsonage still stands in St Peter's Street, but the vicarage in the High Street was replaced by a new house north of the church in 1865.

Following the Tithe Commutation Act of 1836, parishes all over the country were surveyed to work out the exact value of tithes in kind and sums agreed by which individual farmers could buy out their obligation to pay tithes. Marlow's Tithe Map is the first comprehensive large scale map of the parish.

Farming

The farms of Marlow parish are mostly to the north of the town, on the rising ground, with typical Chiltern conditions—thin top soil over chalk with belts of clay and many flints. These flints were, of course, a valuable local building material. There is a considerable contrast between the farms of the corn-growing Thames Valley end of the Chilterns (which includes Marlow) and the Vale of Aylesbury to the north of Buckinghamshire, where traditionally cattle are fattened for Smithfield and which in the 19th century was the greatest butter producing area in England. The Vale of Aylesbury is mainly Kimmeridge and Gault 'blue clay'—heavy strong land—still regarded as wonderful for fattening cattle —but very different from Marlow.

At the time of the 1843 Tithe map, almost the whole of Marlow parish, apart from established woodland, was in arable cultivation. However, large amounts of hay must have been grown to feed the horses, and clover and sainfoin seem to have been part of most farmers' rotation system. Cows were kept in small numbers—mostly in smallholdings in the town, or entirely in stalls. These town dairies died out as transport improved—milk began to be transported over larger distances.

By the 19th century the proportion of Marlow's population directly engaged in agriculture was dropping sharply and, as the century progressed, and imported food became cheap in most areas, farming entered a period of marked depression. By the turn of the century many Marlow farms were without tenants. Some were taken 'in hand' by landowners and some became derelict.

The major landowners for the rural area during the 19th century were the University of Oxford, The Dean and Chapter of Bristol and, of course, the Clayton family. The Williams family owned much of the property in the town but little in the countryside. Very few farmers owned their own land and leases were usually short—leaving no incentive to improve the ground. But the Claytons granted leases up to 14 years with few penalties except in the last three years (most landlords exacted fines from tenants who sold hay or straw off the farm or who ploughed up pasture—in 1815 one writer noted that some tenants were prepared to pay the fines for ploughing pasture 'as the growers of woad will give a great price for sward newly broken from grass').

Some Marlow farmers became famous. Mr. Taylor of Low Grounds was noted for record-breaking cattle—a 1797 print shows his seven-year-old fat steer, which was the wonder of the time!

During the 20th century, the great estates have mostly been broken up and many farms have become owner-occupied. But their size and arrangements had changed very little until recently. In the modern economic climate farms are being sold, subdivided and 'developed' and the old system will soon be unrecognisable. Barmoor is now a small airfield, Holmers and Limmers are almost entirely housing estates, as is also much of the farming land in Marlow Bottom. Foreign ownership is becoming common.

The River

Marlow has grown as a riverside settlement and it is to the river that it owes much of its character and appeal. For many centuries goods were carried by river from Marlow—both up and down stream. Perhaps it was the continual passage of river traffic which led to the local outbreak of the Plague in 1665—in that year 'the some of fifty persones of young and old' were buried. The importance of the river trade is emphasised by the fact that until the mid-19th century the town's High Street led not to a bridge but to the wharves on the river bank. Marlow served as a port for the agricultural products of the southern Chiltern valleys, particularly wood, corn and malt. In 1724, Daniel Defoe recorded that 'it is a town of great embarkation on the Thames, not so much for goods wrought here (for the trade of the town is chiefly in bone lace) but for goods from neighbouring towns and particularly a very great quantity of malt and meal is brought hither from High Wickham, a large market town which is one of the greatest corn markets on this side of England'.

There is also a record of 14,000 bundles of firewood sent down river from Marlow to Southwark by the West Wycombe estate in 1218. This trade became increasingly important as London's demand grew—perhaps it was one reason why woodland was a profitable land use in this area. No doubt some of this firewood found its way into Royal households—Queen Elizabeth I was known to dislike coal. Defoe also noted that at Great Marlow, 'Here is also brought down a vast quantity of beechwood ... a most useful wood ... for billet wood for king's palaces and for glass houses, ... also for fellies (wheel rims) for the Great Carts which ply to London (which are not, by City laws, allowed to have shod wheels) ... and for divers other uses particularly chairmaking and turneryware'.

Thus wood, corn, flour and malt were sent downstream and at the same time coals and rags (for the paper mills) came up from London. The goods were carried in barges hauled by gangs of men, but horses were introduced in the 1770s as the towpath improved —despite riots among the displaced men who eventually received compensation. The barge traffic gradually declined as the railways began to compete for goods traffic in the mid-19th century and today there is very little commercial use of the river, although barges were in occasional use until after the Second World War.

From at least the time of the Conquest, the fisheries of the river were important. The river teemed with eels and the early bridges supported numerous baskets or 'bucks' to catch them. The famous hotel on the Berkshire side of the river is called the *Compleat Angler* but it is doubtful if Isaac Walton ever came to Marlow. The Thames here remains popular with anglers—even salmon are now returning and there is a salmon 'leap' in the modern weir.

The swans of the river appear many times in Marlow history. Grants of their custody are noted in the 15th century and a game of swans (the collective term for a group of swans), with their marks, was left by John Sandes of Great Marlow to his son Henry in 1555. In Henry VIII's time, the penalty for stealing swans' eggs was one year's imprisonment! Ownership of swans is now vested in the Sovereign and the Dyers' and Vintners' Companies, and the colourful ceremony of swan upping still takes place in the third week of July when the cygnets are marked on the beak according to the ownership of the parents.

As late as the last century one of the Cresswell family, who had a farm in Station Road, received payments for taking care of local swans in his yard when the river was frozen.

The Mills

There have been water mills in Marlow at least since the Domesday Survey and to a great extent millers controlled the flow of water. The river meandered along the valley with many shallow places where causeways could be built and carts driven across. To obtain the necessary head of water, the millers installed weirs and sluices—these in turn hindered the river barges and led to continual bad feeling. To allow the passage of boats the old weirs incorporated flash locks (vertical paddles which could be raised to allow boats through). As can be imagined, the resulting 'flash' of water was highly dangerous, particularly for boats going upstream which had to be hauled against the flash by a winch. In Marlow one of these was situated near the bottom of St Peter's Street and there may have been others on the opposite bank. There are many records of the danger of Marlow's flash lock and of the lives lost there. John Taylor, the 16th-century poet, wrote, 'Marlow lock is the worst I must confess, the water is so pinched with shallowness' and in 1585 John Bishop attacked the flash lock owners in a long complaint, also in verse. Marlow lock belonged at that time to a Thomas Farmer, gentleman, a landowner and miller who had taken over the mill previously leased to the Brinkhurst family.

> One ffarmer hath a lock in store
> That hath made many a child to weep
> Their mothers beg from door to door
> Their ffathers drowned in the deep.
>
> At ffarmers lock four men be lost
> Of late I putt you out of doubt
> Three were drowned the stream them toste
> The fourth he had his braines knocked out.

Bishop's complaint was answered by 'those concerned in these locks, wears and mills', saying that the accidents at Marlow were due to barges being badly made, overloaded and without washboards, employing people with no skill and travelling too late and too early—even in winter and on Sundays (the bridge wardens were entitled to levy a fine for working on the Lord's Day).

In the early 18th century, there were three mills in Marlow; a corn mill, an oil mill (processing rape and flax seed) and a mill run by John Lofting (1659-1742) which made brass thimbles. Defoe, writing in the 1720s, enthuses that these were 'excellently well finished'. Lofting came from Holland and had previously had a factory in Islington. He patented a new design of fire engine and one thought to be of his manufacture was presented to Marlow by John Clavering Esq. in 1731—it is still in good repair, lovingly maintained by the local Fire Service. In his memory, John Lofting's sons gave Copy Green Farm (some 79 acres) to support 24 poor boys as apprentices. The charity trustees no longer own the farm but the tradition dies hard. The neighbouring wood at the end of Munday Dean is still known locally as Charity Wood.

By the end of the 18th century, both the oil and the thimble mills had been converted to paper mills. These were later owned and run by the Wright family and employed many local people. The Wrights became prosperous and built substantial houses by the river, near the mills.

There were further mills at Temple on the Berkshire side of the river which employed Marlow labour. Daniel Defoe described their products as 'Bisham Abbey Battery Work, as they call it, viz. brass kettles and pans of all sorts'. In 1788, Thomas Williams, known as the 'Copper Baron' because of his copper mines in Anglesey, bought the Temple Mills and continued to manufacture brass and copper articles there. The copper was brought via the Thames and Severn canal from his smelting works at Swansea. The Williams family used their considerable wealth to buy property in Marlow and thus to control local politics. Members of the family represented Marlow in Parliament for several generations. They built Marlow's Town Hall (now the *Crown Hotel*) using the architect Wyatt who also designed Temple House for the family. Temple House was partly destroyed in a spectacular fire in 1886 and only finally demolished in 1932 after the family fortunes had become eroded.

The Bridges

It is not known when the first bridge over the Thames at Marlow was built, but there are records of a bridge warden in 1227 and of a repair to the bridge in 1294. In 1565 John Semor left 'I oke for 60 years' in his will for bridge repairs. The bridge wardens owned small plots of land, the rents from which, together with the tolls, helped to pay for the upkeep of the bridge.

The present bridge was completed in 1831-2. At least two previous bridges are known; both were wooden and ran from the bottom of St Peter's Street to a point on the opposite bank which is now part of the lawn of the *Compleat Angler*. The earlier of these two bridges was very decrepit by the end of the 18th century and it became necessary to replace it. The County would not contribute to the cost as magistrates ruled that, as there were lands to provide for the bridge, it was not the County's responsibility. Money had to be raised by public subscription, therefore, and a new wooden bridge was built on the old site in 1789. The barge masters requested a large central arch to facilitate the passage of boats. This was raised a further 18 inches after £50 was contributed by the Thames Commissioners.

This bridge was short lived and in 1828 a report on its condition stated that it would be best and cheapest to build a new bridge 'resting on the Buckinghamshire shore at the wharf adjoining the churchyard' and on another wharf on the Berkshire side. The report noted that there would then be a grand entrance to the town and a great improvement in the road on the Berkshire side. The bridge committee considered plans for a wooden bridge, one of stone, and even a cast iron bridge, but the fashionable suspension bridge was chosen. An Act of Parliament 'to defray the expenses of rebuilding Marlow Bridge' was passed in 1829. The Act apportioned the cost as four-fifths to Buckinghamshire and one-fifth to Berkshire, and abolished the office of bridge wardens whose property was to be auctioned. The original engineer, John Millington (1779-1868) left when the work had hardly begun and William Tierney Clark replaced him. Tierney Clark had previously built a suspension bridge at Hammersmith (later demolished) and was to go on to build the bridge over the Danube linking Buda and Pest. This bridge, larger but very similar to that at Marlow, was badly damaged in the last war but has since been rebuilt to the same design.

Three local men did a great deal of the construction work on Marlow Bridge. Mr. Corby was responsible for the brickwork, Mr. William Bond for the timberwork and Mr. Clifford for the stonework. The last named was obviously very proud of his involvement—so much so that his baby daughter, born as the work went on, was christened, on 9 November 1829, Charlotte Suspensiana Clifford. The ironwork was by a William Hazeltine of Shrewsbury. When it was finished, Thomas Rolls (who had a wharf on the river) said in 1832 that it was a 'very pretty thing and a great ornament to the neighbourhood'.

Further work or repairs must have been carried out in 1860 (the date on the roundels below the walkways) and there were further repairs in 1927. After the Second World War, traffic increased and the bridge became congested and unsafe for very heavy vehicles. Plans for an entirely new bridge were proposed. Preservationists were horrified and revived the idea of a by-pass which had originally been proposed in 1932. After much debate the planners were persuaded and in 1972 the new by-pass was opened, crossing the river some way downstream on a new bridge. Major repairs to the old bridge commenced in 1964 and, though it has a five-ton limit, it is now stronger than Tierney Clark could ever have envisaged.

Just up river from the present bridge on the Buckinghamshire side stood the old conventual barn (probably belonging to Bisham Abbey). It was said to be 'in the style of Edward I' but gradually became very dilapidated and was used as a store for coal, probably brought by barges. It was pulled down and the timbers were used in the construction of Lane End church in 1878. During the Napoleonic wars, this and other buildings in the town were used to house French prisoners-of-war. These prisoners were given much freedom in the town but their parole only extended to the small bridge at the foot of Quarry Woods—still known as Parole Bridge.

The Locks

Navigation through Marlow was greatly improved when the old flash lock was replaced in 1773 by a pound lock, in which barges could be safely raised or lowered between two lock gates. The siting of the lock further from the bridge also contributed to greater safety. This first lock was turf sided and required much maintenance. At some later time, the lock was lined with oak, but in 1825 a lock of Headington stone was built and a lock-keeper's house provided. Barges still had to be hauled through the lock—usually by a complicated system of ropes and horses. The toll for the lock was at first one penny, but this was raised to four pence in 1779. (In 1994 the charge for a 'tug' is £2.50 but most boat passages through the locks are now paid for by an annual licence fee.)

Traffic on the river is now mainly for pleasure although powered launches have almost completely replaced the skiffs and punts which carried the fashionable crowd through Marlow lock in the first half of this century.

Water levels are more carefully controlled so that flooding of areas such as St Peter's Street and South Place is no longer common. Perhaps for the same reason we may never see a completely frozen river again. It happened in 1895 when a horse and cart were driven across and a sheep was roasted on the ice!

Markets and Fairs

Marlow's market was established well before 1227-8 when the tradesmen complained at the imposition by the lord of the manor of a halfpenny levy on each measure of corn sold in the market. Cloth was also sold in the market, for in 1241 Richard the dyer of Marlow is mentioned in the Assize Rolls. The reference in the Hundred Rolls to the Earl of Gloucester purchasing a market from the King in about 1260 must relate to a new charter legitimising an existing market. Edward II granted Hugh Spencer the right to hold a fair at his manor of Chepping (i.e. market) Marlow.

The market at Marlow declined to the extent that, in 1600, John Rotheram of Seymours left £40 in his will to purchase a new market. This was unsuccessful, but Thomas Williams of Temple did purchase a market in the 1780s and rebuilt the Market House in 1807. By 1830, however, Kelly's *Directory* described the Saturday market as 'very trifling' and soon after the market lapsed again.

Kelly's *Directory* noted that Marlow's fairs were, however, 'considerable'. They were a horse and cattle fair in May and one for cheese, hops and butter in October. The latter continued until 1903 as a street fair. The town council eventually moved the fair for a few years to a meadow outside the town as the stalls and caravans in the High Street greatly impeded traffic and it had become a jollification rather than a true fair. The old established date had been 29 October and at one time it was a great place for the trading of horses and for farmers to meet and bargain. After the building of the railway, cattle trucks came in by rail to the unloading pens at the end of the line.

The more modern weekly cattle market, down by Marlow station, was held on Mondays, with a Fat Stock Show at Christmas. Many farmers drove their stock to market and also to the many butchers in the town. The market closed in the early 1960s.

The Churches

There has been a church in Marlow since the 12th century—possibly built of clunch (hard chalk). There is an 11th-century record of a visiting Bishop (St Wulfstan) who lost his shoes in the marshy ground and had to be carried into church. The tower was at the rear of the old church and, in the 18th century, the room to the right of the tower was the 'dead house' and the room to the left was for the fire engine. The old church was always liable to flooding and needed frequent repairs. An interesting excerpt from *The Annual Register* for the year 1791 adds colour to the story. The Register, in the section headed 'Chronicle', notes: 'August 7th. William Gray, about 25 years of age, being employed on a scaffold erected for the purpose of painting the spire of Great Marlow church, by the breaking of one of the pullies, fell with part of the scaffold upon the battlements upon the roof of the church, from the roof of the church to the ground, being in the whole full four score feet perpendicular. His right hand was somewhat lacerated, but he had no bone broken or dislocated.'

After the first pound lock was built in 1773, Marlow church was flooded even more regularly. In 1777, braziers were installed (at a cost of six guineas) and said to be 'most comfortable'. In 1809, the water in the church was said to have risen 'over the top step as you go up into the singing gallery'. The second pound lock made matters worse and a survey of the old church in 1830 records 'water marks on the pews about 17 inches above the floor ... The mischievous consequences of such a state of the building to the health of the parties attending worship therein, as well as the injurious effect to the fabric which is extensively covered with a green vegetation are such as to call loudly for an amendment in that particular'. Part of the church collapsed in 1831 and a new building on more or less the same site was built 1832-1835. Again William Bond was a contractor.

The new church was a simple rectangular nave with a small tower and spire. The cost of rebuilding was £15,654 which had to be repaid by a special rate on the parishioners. This was in addition to the existing parish rate to defray church expenses—the cause of much discontent in the town and surrounding parish. In 1865 a vicarage was built just to the north of the church, necessitating the demolition of the old *Swan Inn*. Changes of fashion in church architecture during the 19th century demanded that a chancel was added to the church in 1875 and in 1882 the galleries were removed and arcades erected in the nave. The transformation of the simple preaching-house style church of the 1830s came with the construction of a new high pitched roof in 1889 and the remodelling of the tower and spire in 1898-9. The work of converting the perpendicular-style windows of 1835 to the more acceptable decorated style required the walls to be of greater depth. This work was never completed and the tusking of the bricks next between the original and the altered windows remains to this day.

In the present church porch can be seen the memorial to Sir Miles Hobart. He was one of Marlow's MPs and in 1628 was one of the Members who, during the dispute with the King over ship money, locked the door of Parliament in the face of the messengers of Charles I. He was imprisoned for this and, when released, he was killed in a coach accident on Holborn Hill. The other people who helped to lock the doors were given a pension but as he was dead some of the money was used to erect a monument—perhaps the first monument paid for by public money. The tablet is very graphic and clearly shows the wheel coming off his coach.

In the middle of the 19th century it was felt that the parish church was inadequate and a daughter church was built 'for the larger number of poor persons'. The *Bucks Herald* had reported that the parish church 'is occupied almost exclusively by the wealthier classes' and there were very few free seats. The new church was Holy Trinity, on ground off Dean Street—it was closed in the 1970s as church attendance generally declined.

Marlow has had its share of Catholic 'recusants'—some of whom were brought to court amid fears of Catholic plots in the time of Charles II. Among these were John Farmer and John Brinkhurst, successive owners of Marlow Mills. John Brinkhurst founded a charity in 1608 in Marlow to house poor parishioners. His Almshouses on Oxford Lane stood until 1969 and new housing for old people has replaced them. The tolls from a wharf (near the bottom of St Peter's Street) formed part of the foundation's income.

A Roman Catholic church, however, was eventually built however in St Peter's Street in 1846—to the design of Pugin. The money was found by a private donor and the church served a wide area, including High Wycombe and Maidenhead, despite wide and persistant anti-Catholic feelings.

There had been a strong Nonconformist element in Marlow, but the first church was the Independent Chapel, built in 1726 and replaced by the present building in Quoiting Square in 1840. It now continues as the United Reformed Church. The highly ornate

Wesleyan Chapel in Spittal Street dates from 1900 and replaced a building erected in 1810. There was also a primitive Methodist chapel in Chapel Street built in 1841. The Baptists were also strong, replacing their chapel in 1884 and refronting the building as late as 1932.

Schools

Marlow's most famous school is that founded by Sir William Borlase in 1624 in memory of his son Henry. The original building can still be seen in West Street among the newer extensions. This 'free school', as it was called, was to teach 24 poor boys 'to read and write, and cast accounts' and six were later to be bound as apprentices. There was an adjoining building which was used as a workhouse and in which 24 poor girls were to be taught to 'knit and spin and make bone lace'—no mention of reading and writing for them! The boys wore blue cloaks for church parade on Sundays and were known as Blue Boys. Finances were always difficult and fee-paying pupils were later admitted. After a reorganisation by the charity commissioners and a major building programme, the school reopened as a boys' grammar school in 1881. After the 1902 Education Act, Buckinghamshire County Council was able to provide funds for further building and for scholarships.

The history of the girls' school is patchy and provision for girls lapsed at times. It was revived in 1822 but discontinued some twenty years later when parents no longer wanted their daughters to be taught lacemaking. Payments were made by the free school trustees to enable the girls to attend the National School, therefore, and it was not until 1988 that girls were fully admitted to Sir William Borlase's school.

A National School for boys was established in Marlow in 1813 in a house in Church Passage (one of many in that area which were later demolished to make way for the building of Bridge House). A girls' school was built in 1814. Both schools were funded by subscriptions, each subscriber nominating a child, and special sermons were preached to help to raise money. Later, charges were introduced (one penny a week at first) but funds were always short. By the 1830s, the national school had moved to a building and garden behind the *Crown*.

In 1869 an infants' school opened in St Peter's Street and in 1871 the girls' school moved next to it and remained there even after the infants' school moved to Oxford Road. The National school later moved to the building which is now All Saints' Church Hall, built in 1851 under the terms of the will of the brewer, Thomas Wethered. In 1913, a boys' school opened in Wethered Road; thus there were three Church of England schools which functioned until after the Second World War. As Marlow's population then increased, there was a complete reorganisation and expansion of the school system so that now only two schools remain as Anglican church schools (aided).

In 1866 Bovingdon Green had its own school (the Jemima Cocks Infant School), founded by the Claytons and later becoming a National school. It only closed in the 1930s. A Catholic school was based at first in St Peter's Street—it is now in Prospect Road.

There have been many other schools in the town at various periods—several of them boarding schools. Perhaps some of them catered for the children of Marlow's numerous dissenters, although no record can be found of a British school, nor was a school board set up after the 1870 Education Act, as was the case in many towns of this size.

Adult Education received much attention during the 19th century. There was a Mutual Improvement Society and, later, as was fashionable, an Institute. This was an attempt to provide further education and to meet the literary and scientific needs of the town. The organisation itself had existed since 1853, but the new Institute building was raised as a local commemoration of Queen Victoria's Golden Jubilee. The adjoining building (to house the 1st Bucks Volunteer Rifles) was built at the same time. General Owen Williams MP, of Temple House, gave the site and funds were raised locally. The Institute was not sectarian, religious or political. There was hope of University extension courses. Later other opportunities for education opened up and the Institute became largely recreational. Television sounded the death knell and it was finally closed in 1957 when the County Council bought the building for use as a library.

Parliamentary Representation and Local Government

Marlow was first represented in Parliament in 1299 in the reign of Edward I (who decreed that there should be two representatives from every borough in the land). However by 1308 it was found to be too expensive to maintain the two members and the practice lapsed. In the reign of James I, Marlow, together with Wendover and Amersham, petitioned to have the right to send members to Parliament restored. James I did not like the idea— he considered he was troubled by too many burgesses already. However the petition was eventually granted in 1622 and Marlow sent two members to Parliament.

The Civil War

During the Civil War, Marlow must have been prey to soldiers from both sides taking what provisions and horses they could find. As a town mid-way between the Parliamentary stronghold of London and the King's base at Oxford, it was in something of a no man's land between the two. The Royalists fortified Greenlands House at nearby Hambleden in order to control traffic along the Thames. The Parliamentarians under Colonel Browne laid siege to the house which only fell in July 1644 after constant bombardment from the Berkshire side of the river.

In Marlow the Parliamentary forces certainly built fortifications in St Peter's Street (to protect the river crossing) and the bridge was partially demolished. The soldiers must have been quartered in the church as the churchwardens' accounts in 1643 mention a payment to Goodwife Langley for 'making clean the church where the soldiers lay'. There is also a record of payments for taking down the bulwarks around the church and in Duck Lane. When Charles I was brought through Marlow as a prisoner in 1647, the church bells were rung and the bellringers were paid five shillings for the task.

The Reform Act

Great Marlow continued to send two MPs to Parliament until the 1832 Reform Act, when the boundaries of the parliamentary borough were extended to include Little Marlow, Medmenham and Bisham. In 1867, the number of representatives was reduced to one. The object of enlarging the borough in 1832 had been to make it harder for the election to be influenced by one landlord, but the Williams family, as the largest employer, dominated elections from the late 18th century right up until Marlow was disfranchised by the Redistribution of Seats Act of 1885. It is now part of Wycombe constituency.

Before 1832 only those men who paid the church rate were entitled to vote—about 250 people. After the Reform Act of 1832, all adult males who owned or occupied property worth at least £10 per year became eligible to vote—thus doubling the electorate. For the first time, proper lists of voters were compiled, but the system was still open to abuse as poll books listing which way individuals had voted were published by the rival parties after the election. The secret ballot was not introduced until the election of 1874.

Until the late 18th century, the Clayton family, as lords of the manor, had regarded Marlow as their pocket borough, encouraging the electorate to support the family candidate by maintaining low rents on their property in the town. With the sale of much of that property to Thomas Williams, the new owner of Temple Mills, Marlow had a patron with even stronger parliamentary ambitions. Owen and Thomas Williams, the Tory candidates in the 1826 election, were closely challenged by James Morrison, a wealthy Londoner championing the Whig cause. They responded by evicting many of their tenants who had voted for Morrison. In 1830 and 1831, the father and son scraped home against Sir William Clayton, but with the death of Owen Williams soon after the 1831 election, Clayton was returned unopposed. As the 19th century progressed, feeling often ran high in the town where elections were concerned. The main parties were known as the 'Blues' (or reformers), supporting the Claytons of Harleyford, and the 'Coppers' (conservatives) supporters of the Williams's of Temple allied with the Wethered brewing family. On one occasion, windows were smashed at the *Crown* (the Williams's campaign headquarters) and at Wethered's Brewery, and trees on the road to Thomas Wethered's house, Seymour Court, were uprooted. The riot was only quelled after the military had been called out from Windsor. A dent on the casing of the clock above the *Crown* is said to have been caused at this time.

Local Government

Before the 19th century, Great Marlow affairs were largely in the hands of the church vestry which concerned itself not only with the church but with the secular matters of the parish, including the upkeep of roads, appointment of constables, collection of rates, and relief of the poor. The vestry had taken up these responsibilities as the old manorial and hundred courts declined from the 16th century onwards.

In the early 20th century, Marlow still had a great deal of autonomy. Marlow Urban District Council was formed in 1896, leaving the rest of the old parish as 'Great Marlow'. M.U.D.C. was responsible for all local services except those provided by the county. It had, for example, a considerable house building programme, acting after the First World War as the agent for building Lloyd George's 'homes fit for heroes'. Council house building continued after the Second World War when some extremely high quality houses were built in the Dean Street area.

After the local government changes in 1974, Marlow became part of Wycombe District with Marlow Town Council as a third tier (parish) council, retaining the right to elect a town mayor.

Public Services

The Marlow gas works was situated on the west side of Dean Street. It was, of course, coal-fired and entailed many hours of shovelling coke, drawing off tar and so on. Great Marlow's gas company was founded in 1845, gas lighting was introduced to the main street in 1848 and only replaced by electricity in the 1930s. The gas works expanded to fill a three-acre site in 1898 and only closed in 1951.

The waterworks began with a proposal in 1883 to 'sink a well and supply mains water'. The pumping station is still in Chalkpit Lane, with a reservoir at Bovingdon Green, and its potential supply was always in excess of that needed by the town—a very desirable feature when nationalisation took place.

Marlow's sewers date from the early 20th century. In 1929 there was a great ceremony when the chairman of the old M.U.D.C. 'turned the first sod' with a special silver spade to mark the beginning of the council's main drainage system. Before that time the cesspits and earth closets behind the houses needed regular 'servicing' and the carts were a familiar sight. Many summonses were issued for 'cesspit nuisances' including one, in 1848, addressed to the trustees of the Free School (Sir William Borlase's) referring to a 'full, foul and offensive' cesspit at the cottages in Chapel Street belonging to the school. The old Marlow sewage works (just beyond the old Marlow station) has now been replaced by a modern system out towards Bourne End which serves a larger area.

Law and Order

Prior to the establishment of the county police forces, law and order were enforced in Marlow by locally appointed constables. A Marlow constable's baton from the reign of William IV is still in existence. The 17th-century court records mention prosecutions of Marlow men for assault, for stealing and for poaching and of a woman for being a scold. In 1698, Thomas Stapers, a convicted thief, was whipped at the cart's tail from the Market Place to the *Three Tuns* and back. The wrongdoers were often bargemen—they must have been a rough lot—and there is a nice story of bargemen stealing pies from a riverside inn until the landlady used newly killed puppies to fill some pies—which were stolen in due course, causing shouts of 'who stole puppy pies under Marlow Bridge'!

Sometimes the constables themselves fell from grace—on one occasion a constable falsely 'set a man in the stocks in the public Market Place' as the result of a grudge! Marlow's stocks were removed from the Market Place in 1876 and were displayed by the causeway. They are now in the County Museum in Aylesbury. The office of Parish Constable disappeared in 1872. The County Police were formed in 1857 and Marlow had one of the first police stations, built in 1869. It was in Trinity Road and also housed the Magistrates Court. Marlow Court has now been merged with that for Wycombe District.

The Workhouse

Before the Poor Law Amendment Act of 1834 the relief of the poor, in Marlow as in every other parish, was derived from Elizabethan laws. Many people endowed charities, as John Brinkhurst had done, to help apprentices, or to provide warm flannel gowns or pay small sums of money to widows and other needy people. Lists of some of these benefactors may still be seen in the church porch. Overseers of the poor were appointed who levied a poor rate on the parish and gave money to poor families to carry on living in their own homes or accommodated them in a parish workhouse where work such as cultivation or weaving was provided.

The house next to Sir William Borlase's school was The House of Correction, Marlow's first workhouse, but by the middle of the 18th century a new workhouse had been built in Berwick Road. Samuel Richardson, the great showman, was born there in 1766. He is buried in All Saints' churchyard. Most of the workhouse building still stands —converted into houses.

After 1834, parishes were joined in unions for the purposes of poor relief and Marlow became part of Wycombe Union with a new Union workhouse at Saunderton. The arrangement was resisted in Marlow where people preferred independence—a facet of Marlow character not unknown today!

Transport

Trade in Marlow was always dominated by the river but, until the turnpike era, pack animals were the principal means of transport. Carts and wagons became more common only as the roads improved. As Wycombe's furniture industry developed, great wagons loaded with chairs were a frequent sight in Marlow. At least one popular waggoner's inn had to have the arch above the entry to the yard raised to allow in the wagons piled high with chairs. In 1555, the responsibility for the upkeep of roads was laid clearly on the parishes and did not change until the County Councils of 1889 took them over. It was the 'vestry' authorities who, on behalf of the parish, administered road maintenance and every man had to contribute by money or labour to the upkeep of the parish roads. In this district the road surfaces were very poor and often repaired with flints which, being brittle, became pulverised under the weight of traffic. The 1555 Act of Parliament provided for the appointment of official surveyors elected locally, but this does not seem to have been done in Marlow until 1671. The roads improved only gradually.

In the early 18th century, turnpike trusts were established, enabling local gentry and tradesmen to form committees empowered to collect tolls on main roads and apply the receipts to the repair of the surface. To the south of Marlow, the Bath Road through Maidenhead was turnpiked in 1718. It had a branch to Henley. To the north, the Oxford Road through High Wycombe and Stokenchurch was turnpiked in 1719. The size of wagon loads increased greatly and the new speed of trade led to changes in local agriculture as new markets opened up. Meat and grain now went further afield. Transport of coal became easier, so the great market for firewood diminished and local woods were no longer coppiced. Luckily, the growth of the furniture industry around High Wycombe preserved our woods and they were converted to the beautiful tall beech woods we know today.

An Act of Parliament of 1768 provided for the turnpiking of the road from Hatfield to Reading, passing through Amersham and High Wycombe. At Marlow the main route continued to Henley, but the Act included the alternative route over Marlow Bridge to the 30th milestone on the Bath Road. The obelisk erected in 1822 by the turnpike trustees in Marlow Market Square gives the distances to Hatfield via High Wycombe (36), Reading via Henley (15) and Reading via Marlow Bridge (14). There was a toll-house in Chapel Street and another local one near Greenlands on the way to Henley. In 1826, the charges at the tollhouse in Chapel Street were 4d. for a horse and carriage, cattle 10d. a score and sheep and pigs 5d. a score. There were some exceptions—mail coaches passed free as did parish traffic, clergymen on duty (except itinerant preachers such as John Wesley), soldiers on the march, persons passing to funerals or places of worship and horses carrying vagrants (which had to be officially returned to their own parishes).

The Marlow to Stokenchurch road was turnpiked in 1791—and the stone milestones can still be seen on the road to Lane End. Before the turnpike act, the original road reached the top of Seymour Court Hill from the direction of Seymour Plain. The turnpike trustees diverted the road to leave the town via Dean Street (previously the road to Munday Dean only). This route is referred to as the 'new road to Oxford' on an 1801 map of land belonging to the church. Local tradition has credited Thomas Owen Wethered with making this diversion. He purchased Seymour Court in 1862 and his planting of trees lining the road, possibly an attempt to provide work for unemployed labourers at this time, may have given rise to the story.

The turnpike roads made fast travel by coach more practical and Marlow was well served by coaching inns. The *Lower Crown* (the site of the present Lloyds Bank in the High Street) was the departure point for the 'Flier' which left Marlow twice daily for

London but the *Greyhound* (in Spittal Street) and the *Crown* in Market Square were also coaching inns, and the *Horns* in Chapel Street was the start of a wagon service to London. In the 18th century the mail coaches passed through High Wycombe, from which there was a bye-post to Marlow each day. In the 19th century, Maidenhead became the post town, with a mail cart bringing the post to Marlow. After the railway came to Maidenhead in 1838, a coach called 'the Wonder' ran from the *Crown* to connect with the trains on the Great Western Railway,

Thomas Williams, who had purchased Marlow's market rights from the Claytons in the 1780s, endeavoured to revive local trade by building a new Market House on land adjoining the *Crown*. The old wooden structure in the Market Square was pulled down and a substantial new structure planned. His son, Owen Williams, completed the work in 1807. The building had three open arches to the ground floor level and a grand assembly or meeting room on the first floor. The clock, made by W. N. & N. Lawton of Newton le Willows, Lancashire, was presented by Pascoe Grenfell, friend of the Williams family and MP for Marlow 1807-1820. The adjoining *Crown* eventually took over the Assembly Room and in the 1880s the building ceased to be a market house and became of the *Crown*. The arches were enclosed and at one time housed the town's lock-up.

In the early 20th century, the town's fire engine was kept in part of the market house. Marlow's voluntary fire brigade was always a feature of the town, the service having existed for almost three hundred years. The engine was horse-drawn until after the First World War—the horses were kept in the field behind what is now the *Crown Hotel*. The brigade was summoned by a bell on top of the hotel. In 1925, the horse-drawn engine was replaced by the famous powered Dennis engine which was christened 'Vera' in honour of Lady Terrington (who had subscribed generously to the purchase fund). This engine was in use until the Second World War and even went to London during the blitz.

The Railway

In 1872, the privately funded Great Marlow Railway Company was formed to provide a spur to join the Maidenhead to High Wycombe branch of the Great Western Railway at Bourne End. A fine station was built, but the building was demolished in 1968 to facilitate the development of the industrial estate. Despite several threats of closure, the line remains open.

The greatest change in Marlow's transport system has come with the building of the M4 and M40 motorways—making journeys by car to London and to the West and the Midlands easy and fast. Marlow has grown tremendously as a result and changed from a tightly-knit community with small businesses to one of commuters, offices, and supermarkets. Population growth in Marlow had previously been slow and the town had lagged behind such centres as Wycombe, Maidenhead and Slough. In the early 19th century the population numbered about 3,000—it grew slowly to about 5,000 in 1950 but today is nearer 20,000. With the coming of the by-pass and the further widening and extension of the motorways, who will recognise the Marlow of the 21st century?

Industry

'Partly agricultural and partly manufacturing.' This was how Thomas Rolls described the town in 1840. He was the treasurer of the feoffees (or governors) of Sir William Borlase's school in Marlow and was applying to the Ironmongers' Company for financial help for the school from Betton's charity, administered by the Company. Mr. Rolls' description emphasises the change that must have been taking place in the town by the 19th century. No longer completely dependent on agriculture and river transport, the local economy now rested partially on employment at the mills, and in the brewery, in small local factories and in the gas works and other services.

Brewing must always have been carried out in Marlow. In the 18th century, there was a brewer in St Peter's Street named John Gibbons. His daughter married a George Wethered in 1744 and it was George who founded the famous brewery probably on the east side of the High Street. His son Thomas moved the business, to the west side of Marlow High Street. One of the brewery's greatest assets was the water from its own artesian well. The brewery continued to be associated with the Wethered family, until after the Second World War when it was taken over by Strong's of Romsey and then by Whitbreads. The brewery closed in 1988—the end of an era in Marlow. But the elegant Georgian houses of the Wethered family, which were later used as brewery offices, remain to front the High Street.

Local building firms become important as the town grew. Y.J. Lovell took over the long-established business of Messrs. Corby in 1876 and remained a major employer in the town until after the Second World War. Wood for their timber yard came in by barge.

Other industries in the town were on a very small scale and often cottage-based. There was a small chair factory in St Peter's Street and chair seats were caned nearby. Rope-making as an occupation declined as the barge trade became less important but, skewer and peg making continued into this century particularly in Dean Street and among the gypsies of the area. There was a local pottery and brick kiln at Bovingdon Green and a small workshop in West Street making children's bibs and embroidered items.

But the cottage industry for which the town had become well-known was the making of bone lace. There were lace schools where girls were taught the intricate patterns and this was also done in the workhouse, but the majority of the work was done as piece work in the cottages and was very badly paid. Lace-making probably came to this country in the 15th century, perhaps with Flemish weavers, and flourished in Buckinghamshire until the advent of machine-made lace, in Nottingham and elsewhere, rendered the hand-made product uneconomic. The lace made in Buckinghamshire was pillow lace where bobbins were moved over a pad where the pattern was laid out with pins. The bobbins were often of bone and beautifully carved and decorated. They became family heirlooms.

As the market for bone lace declined, the workers turned to embroidery on net and satin stitch work. Part of the trousseau of Queen Victoria's eldest daughter Vicky was trimmed with embroidered net from Marlow.

Opportunities for bettering oneself were few and many men looked further afield. There is a touching account of a farewell walk to Munday Dean Farm, by a man from a family still well known in Marlow, before he went to London to join a group emigrating to the Cape of Good Hope in 1819. It is a reflection of the lack of opportunity for working-class families at this time.

The Streets

Marlow's street pattern is T-shaped, formed by the junction at the top of the High Street of the east-west road from High Wycombe to Henley, with the north-south road leading from High Wycombe to Reading. West Street and the High Street were to some extent brought up to date in Georgian times—often by rebuilding the façades, so that many of the buildings are much older at the back than at the front! Several reveal evidence of Elizabethan work and some, perhaps, of the 15th century. This is also true of other parts of the town—in fact St Peter's Street has what is probably the oldest building in the town—the Old Parsonage whose central hall dates from the early 14th century. It may have been the residence of the rector until 1494, when it was given to Tewkesbury Abbey, but the abbot and his successors, the Dean and Chapter of Gloucester, leased the house, and employed a vicar to look after the spiritual needs of Marlow.

St Peter's Street, of course, was important for many centuries as the road that led to the bridge. It seems to have been called by various names, including Bridge Street and Duck Lane. The name St Peter's Street or 'Peter Street' appears on various old maps and in directories published well before the Roman Catholic church was built in 1846. Perhaps the church was named after the street and not the other way round, as is usually supposed.

One of the more distinguished 18th-century buildings in the High Street is Cromwell House (known earlier as Alfred House) which, until 1991, was Marlow's post office. During the time the Military College was at Remnantz, this and many other buildings in the town housed cadets. Later, Edwin Clark the famous civil engineer lived here. Clark, born in Marlow the son of a manufacturer of pillowlace, was a man of great talent, responsible for major engineering projects all over the world, but not too proud to act as consulting engineer for Marlow's humble branch railway. The inside of Cromwell House has been much modified but the enormous carved overmantel and fireplace remains in what used to be the postmaster's office. It is said to have been carved by French prisoners held in Marlow during the Napoleonic wars.

The most imposing façade in West Street is that of Remnantz, probably built by Stephen Remnant, an armaments manufacturer from Woolwich, who lived there in the 18th century. The Royal Military Academy established its junior section there in 1801-2 and cadet training continued there for some 11 years. There is a famous picture of the cadets in their red uniforms parading before the Duke of York and distinguished guests. In addition to Remnantz, several houses within the town provided accommodation for the cadets, including Marlow Place and Cromwell House. The boys had to rise early and work late—the conditions were so bad at one stage that there was a mutiny by about nine boys, who were later expelled. The establishment moved to Sandhurst in 1812. Many of the houses which had been used by the Military College were in a sad state of disrepair in 1814 and were without tenants. Remnantz was later occupied by the Wethered family, owners of the brewery.

The poet Shelley lived in a house on the north side of West Street from 1817-18 with his second wife Mary Godwin—author of the first science fiction novel, *Frankenstein*. Shelley came here perhaps as a result of his friendship with Thomas Peacock, another writer, who, at one time, lived in West Street opposite Quoiting Square (the house is now a shop). During his stay Shelley wrote *The Revolt of Islam*. He led a dreamy life in Marlow, often lying in a boat floating on the river. He befriended the poor—despite his debts—and was even known to have given away his shoes. From Marlow he went to Italy where he was drowned in 1822.

Spittal Street's name is probably derived from the old hospice of St Thomas, a travellers' rest known to have existed in Marlow in 1384. What we now call Spittal Square used to be named the Common Slough. Chapel Street must have been named after the chantry chapel known to have been founded here in the medieval period. The name does not come from the Primitive Methodist chapel, which was not built until 1841.

Dean Street must have developed from a medieval track into the Chiltern Hills and has always been full of character. It has been largely rebuilt, in stages before and after the last war. Previously the cottages and tenements housed large numbers of Marlow's poorer people—many of them labourers on the farms, at the brewery or the gas works and elsewhere. The houses were 'two deep', with narrow alleys behind the street front. It was well provided with public houses and ale houses (over twenty before the first war) and was popularly known as 'the City' as three of the 'pubs' were *The Bank of England*, the *Royal Exchange* and the *Mint*! It was a rough area and police were said to patrol only in pairs. Up to the 1930s there was a gypsy encampment at the top and many residents of the area were didicoys (part-gypsies).

Station Road was not named as such, of course, until after the coming of the railway. It was previously known as Brook Street and Institute Road did not exist until the Institute (now the library) was built in 1890.

At the turn of the century there was much housing development in the area between the High Street and Glade Road. This continued after the building of the new hospital—opened by General Higginson in 1915. The original hospital had grown out of a merger between the Sick Aid Depot and the Nursing Fund Committee and had opened in 1889 in Cambridge House, Cambridge Road, with the famous Sister Cole in charge. In 1910-11 it was realised that it was too small and inconvenient and once again public subscriptions were called for. The new site, off Glade Road, was donated and the building was the beginning of our present Community Hospital.

Between the wars, development continued slowly—the Newtown Road area and Lock Road date from this time. House building was largely free from planning restraints until after the last war but then, despite the restrictions, it developed rapidly. The largest housing estates—both the privately-developed areas to the west and the council-built estates to the north and east, began in the 1950s and 1960s.

The two valleys to the north of the town developed differently. Both Marlow Bottom Road and Munday Dean Lane were largely unspoiled lanes—leading to farms and woodland—until the 1930s. Both then suffered the intrusion of cheaply built 'shacks', mostly serving as weekend homes for people from London and elsewhere as the motor-car began to make this possible. Marlow Bottom, in particular, grew further as wartime bombing made the cities unsafe and after the war the growth there just mushroomed as proper houses replaced the old shacks and tin-roofed shanties. There is now a school, a small church, a few shops and many side roads. Munday Dean has been largely preserved. Plans to develop Munday Dean Farm into a housing estate never came to fruition. Some pre-war bungalows remain and there are now a few houses, but the beautiful winding valley remains largely unspoilt.

Leisure and Sport

There was a racecourse in Marlow for at least 100 years. There is a vivid account of a visit to Marlow Races in the *Gentleman's Magazine* of 1752. The two-day event was held in August down by the river in the Gossmore/Riverwoods area and no gambling devices were allowed on the course! It closed in 1847.

But interest in sport has always been a feature in Marlow. The regatta is famous and its records date back to 1855 although it only became a fully organised event after 1865—starting in alternate years with Maidenhead. At first the event was associated with a carnival but there were complaints at the lack of serious rowing. No-one could say that today!

Marlow Football Club began in 1870 and was one of the first 15 subscribers to the F.A. Cup. They have never missed a year in entering for the cup—a record not equalled by any other club in the country! In 1882 they reached the semi finals! Marlow Rugby Club officially dates from 1947 but there was a team in 1913 who beat Wycombe 13-0.

Marlow Cricket Club dates from 1829 but there was a long gap from 1920 to 1950 when it was reformed. Marlow Park cricket club is a separate organisation.

During the last century, if not before, social life in Marlow was full of interest, at least for the better off. Balls were held (in the meeting room on the first floor of the *Crown*). There were flower shows, meets of the local hunt, and concerts and lectures were regularly held—often associated with local fund-raising for good causes such as the hospital or Institute.

Most of Marlow's other clubs are of recent foundation and all sorts of sporting and leisure amenities, both indoor and out, are now available, many associated with Court Garden Leisure Centre.

The story of how the town came to possess Court Garden and the adjoining parkland began with the initiative of public-spirited local people. The house was originally built in 1758 for a distinguished physician specialising in nervous diseases. His name was Dr. Battie! In the early 1920s the estate was due to be sold and there was a distinct possibility of its division into small plots for riverside homes. A group of local men began fundraising and had the brilliant idea of associating the fund with the hundredth birthday of the man who was at that time Marlow's most famous citizen. This was General Sir George Higginson—a Crimean War veteran, 'the father of the Brigade of Guards' and a personal friend of the Royal family. His involvement widened the list of subscribers—among whom was the General himself—and in 1926 the estate was purchased. At a great ceremony attended by Princess Mary (the Princess Royal), the General's god-daughter, the keys were handed to the General and he presented them to the town, as the band of his old regiment, the Grenadier Guards, played. So it is to the far-sighted citizens of 1926 that we owe that enormous asset to the town, Higginson Park and Court Garden. The house was administered by Trustees and at first it was partly leased to Marlow Urban District Council who took it over completely in 1955. It is now run by Wycombe District Council after the changes in local government of 1974.

Like most small towns, Marlow is fiercely independent. Its interests are now represented by Marlow Town Council for the urban area and Great Marlow Parish Council for the rural area. Whilst their areas of responsibility are relatively modest, these councils are consulted on planning and other major issues and their powers are likely to be enhanced in the future.

1 At the Conquest, the valuable manor of Marlow was given to William's queen, Matilda. Her own farm there had two ploughs; 58 tenant farmers had a further 24 ploughs and there was enough meadow land to provide feed for the 200 or more oxen required to pull these ploughs.

2 Great Marlow manor house appears to have stood in the lower end of the High Street. It was reduced in status because later lords of the manor preferred to live at the nearby manor of Harleyford. The Court House or Manor House with a three-acre close behind is listed in the sale of the manor to Sir William Clayton in 1735.

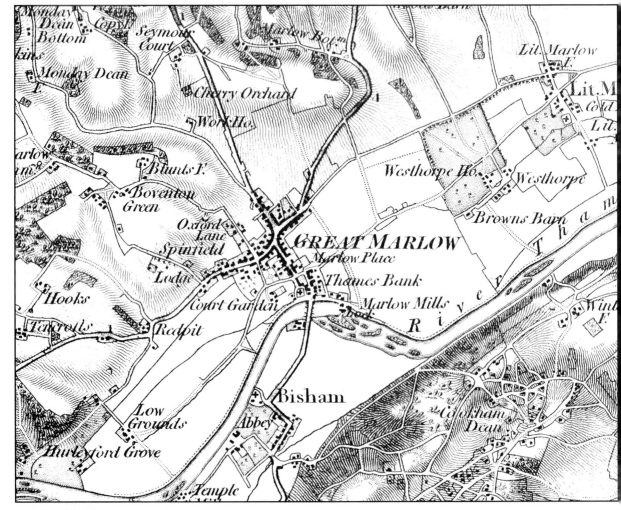

3 The large number of ploughs listed in Domesday Book suggests that Marlow's open fields, to the east and north of the present town, had already been laid out. Each farmer had a number of strips of land in each field and planted and harvested his crops at the same time as his neighbour. This 1822 Ordnance Survey map marks the boundaries of the surviving open fields and shows the roads crossing them as unfenced.

4 Not all Marlow's farmers lived in the town. The upland farmsteads like Hooks Farm are ancient settlements which were never brought into the open-field system. In a 1717 list, Hooks Farm extends to 80 acres let to a Richard Corbee at £35 per year.

5 Widmere, another upland farmstead, has been associated with a second Marlow manor listed in Domesday as belonging to Walter Vernon.

6 Widmere evidently developed early into a hamlet, for a chapel was built here in the 13th century. By the 17th century it had been converted into housing with a first floor inserted, but the mouldings of 14th-century windows on the south wall are clearly visible.

7 The crypt beneath the chapel at Widmere was for many years used as a dairy for the farm. It is in two aisles and vaulted in square bays supported by three circular pillars.

8 Low Grounds Farm, shown here before its recent conversion, was built on the valley bottom in the early 18th century. The Marlow historian Thomas Langley, in a manuscript family history, states that Low Grounds was originally farmed from a house at the southern end of the High Street which was 'new fronted' in about 1760.

9 Low Grounds Farm has a huge timber-framed barn with two cart entrances. It is probably of mid-18th-century date.

10 Harvest time at Cold Harbour, Seymour Court Farm, in the 1930s. The horses are pulling a binder which cuts the wheat and leaves the sheaves.

11 Threshing at Widmere Farm in the 1930s. Sheaves of wheat are taken from the ricks and from the Dutch barn and fed into a threshing machine powered by belt from a tractor.

12 At Domesday the manor of Marlow had a mill worth 20s. per year, suggesting that there was already a weir across the river diverting the flow over its water-wheel. All tenants would be obliged to grind their corn at the mill.

13 The Domesday manor also enjoyed the profits of 1,000 eels per year, probably caught in eel bucks such as these shown attached to the weir in this early print.

14 (*top left*) By 1279 the town of Marlow was flourishing and the names of nearly 200 tradesmen are given in the Hundred Rolls. Here they are called 'burgesses', suggesting that streets had been laid out with house plots entitling the occupiers to take part in civic affairs.

15 (*above*) Marlow's success in medieval times surely came from its position as a trading post and a crossing point on the Thames. As early as 1218 there is record of 14,000 bundles of firewood from West Wycombe being sent down river from Marlow. Here a barge is being loaded with timber in the late 19th century.

16 (*left*) In 1227 there is evidence that a bridge warden was applying the income from lands to the repair of a bridge over the Thames at Marlow. Early prints of Marlow show not the medieval bridge but a replacement built entirely of wood in 1789. It crossed the river downstream from the church on the line of St Peter's Street.

17   St Peter's Street was until 1832 the road to the bridge and was lined with houses and cottages occupied by bargemen, wharfingers, coal porters, brewers' labourers and workers at the paper mills. At the bottom of the street were the *Two Brewers* and the *Watermans Arms* beerhouse.

18   An early view of St Peter's Street taken from the weir. The cottages on the left were demolished about 1872 when Old Bridge House was built on the site.

19 The bridge was found to be in need of extensive repair or replacement in the 1820s. A private Act of Parliament was passed in 1829 'for raising money to defray the expenses of rebuilding Marlow Bridge'. The new bridge was sited on the line of High Street, some way upstream from the old bridge. It was completed in 1832 at a cost of £22,000.

20 Having rejected designs for conventional timber or stone bridges, and one for a single-span bridge of cast iron, the promoters decided on a fashionable suspension bridge. Early on in the project, the original engineer, John Millington (1779-1868), was replaced by William Tierney Clark (1783-1852) who is best known for the building of a suspension bridge over the Danube at Budapest, completed in 1849.

21 Successive repairs burdened Clark's structure with an ever increasing weight of tarmac. The bridge is shown here under repair, probably in 1927.

2 The suspension bridge was largely rebuilt between 1964 and 1966. The iron chains were replaced with steel and the heavy tarmac road surface replaced by durable metal plates. The opening of the Marlow by-pass with a new Thames bridge in 1972 has taken the weight of traffic off the suspension bridge.

3 A 1794 directory describes how '... the Thames brings goods hither from the neighbouring towns, especially great quantites of meal and malt from High Wycombe, and beech from several parts of the county'. In the 19th century boats coming upstream brought a variety of merchandise, especially coal, which was unloaded at the wharf where an old barn stood until the 1870s.

24 This early 19th-century print looking from the Berkshire side of the old bridge shows a barge near the wharf at the end of St Peter's Street. In the background is the house called Thames Bank with its luxuriant garden sloping down to the river.

25 Boats could only descend the weir on a flash of water created by raising a gate in the centre. Boats coming upstream were hauled through the flash lock by a rope attached to a huge capstan on the wharf. Flash locks wasted water and boats often capsized in the surge of unleashed water.

26 A pound lock, having two sets of gates between which a boat could be lowered or raised efficiently and safely, was built at the end of the weir, next to Marlow Mills, in 1773. Its dimensions were 110 ft. by 18 ft.

27 The original pound lock, which had walls of turf, was replaced by this stone-built lock and lock keeper's house in 1825. The lock was again rebuilt in 1927.

28 The lock gates were manually operated until the 1960s. These well-dressed men, out for a stroll, are standing by the footboards which helped those pushing open the gates to gain some purchase.

29 Daniel Defoe, writing in the 1720s, was most impressed by the mills which stood either side of the Marlow corn mill, 'both extraordinary in themselves, one for making thimbles, a work extremely well finished ... another for pressing of oyl from rape seed, and flax seed'. This estate map of 1753 shows the three mills and also the flash lock in the weir and the capstan on the wharf.

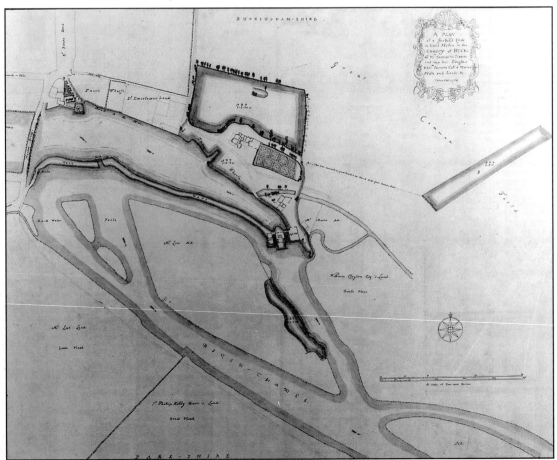

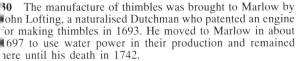

30 The manufacture of thimbles was brought to Marlow by John Lofting, a naturalised Dutchman who patented an engine for making thimbles in 1693. He moved to Marlow in about 1697 to use water power in their production and remained here until his death in 1742.

31 John Lofting had patented a new type of fire engine in 1690. This fire engine, presented to Marlow in 1731 and still maintained at the local fire station, is thought to be made by John Lofting.

32 By the late 18th century the thimble and oil mills had been converted into paper mills run by the Wright family. Their mills were rebuilt in 1825 after a fire, thought to have been started deliberately by those fearing that new machinery would destroy their jobs. Thomas Blizzard of Little Marlow was one of the rioters who in 1830 attacked paper mills in High Wycombe. He was sentenced to death but reprieved after a public campaign to spare him.

33 (*right*) The Wright family prospered and built fine houses on Mill Lane. From left to right they are named The Sycamores, The Garth and Weir Cottage.

34 (*below*) The corn mill was last operated by Stephen Smith in the early years of this century, but the paper mills were worked by the Wright family until 1935. Here the mills are photographed from the footbridge to the lock in 1938.

35 (*below*) The mills were finally demolished in 1965. The site is now occupied by riverside houses whose weatherboard cladding imitates the construction of the mills.

36 Daniel Defoe was equally impressed by the Temple Mills on the Berkshire side of the river in the parish of Bisham. Here he saw a foundry where '... they convert copper into brass, and then, having cast the brass in large broad plates, they beat them out by force of great hammers, wrought by the water mills, into what shape they think fit for sale'.

37 In 1788, Temple Mills were bought by Thomas Williams, owner of copper mines in Anglesey and smelting works in Swansea. Temple Mills employed about fifty men in 1810. Williams employed the architect Samuel Wyatt to design this fine house overlooking the river. Temple House was demolished in 1932.

38 A walk upstream to Temple Lock was a favourite Sunday afternoon pastime. The towpath on the Buckinghamshire side of the river terminated here and a ferry enabled pedestrians and towing horses to continue along the Berkshire bank. A foot bridge has now been built here.

39 With so much malt being shipped from Marlow for use by London brewers it is natural that local maltsters should have become brewers themselves. The *Two Brewers* belonged to Joseph Plumridge who is listed in 1794 as a brewer and maltster. The Gibbons family were also based in St Peter's Street and employed five men in their brewery in 1851.

40 George Wethered married Elizabeth Gibbons in 1744 and set up as a brewer in the High Street. The earliest of many datestones to be found around the brewery site is TW 1788 (referring to his son Thomas Wethered) on a wing at the back of this building. Thomas Wethered's son Owen was living here in 1851; at the time of the census he was employing 47 men in the brewery.

41 Thomas Wethered leased and later purchased this fine home to the north of the brewery site called the White House. Owen Wethered lived here for a time.

42 Thomas Wethered is regarded as the founder of Wethered's Brewery. When he died in 1849, aged 88, he left a fortune of £100,000 and his brewery was producing 24,500 barrels a year.

43 Thomas Wethered lived the later part of his life at Remnantz, a large house on West Street. From 1802-1812 it served as the junior department of the Royal Military College which then removed to Sandhurst.

44 An early photograph shows the proprietor and workmen outside the brewery.

45 (*above*) Some impression of the scale of Wethered's Brewery can be gained from this view of the store.

46 (*above*) The growth of a brewery depended on the acquisition and supply of as many tied houses as possible. By 1872, Wethered's Brewery owned or leased over 100 pubs in Buckinghamshire alone. Here two of the firm's lorries are shown in the brewery yard.

47 (*left*) Competition from other breweries was intense. *The Bank of England* beerhouse on Dean Street, Marlow was one of five pubs in the town owned by Weller's Brewery of Amersham.

48 Marlow's principal inn was the *Crown*, a fine early 18th-century building at the head of the High Street. A coach left the *Crown* and went via Maidenhead and Slough to London every day except Sunday. On this photograph the tall central archway leading to the stable yard is prominent and the assembly room of the Town Hall has been taken over by the inn.

49 The *Crown* took over the covered market under the arches of the Town Hall and later sold the original building for conversion into shops.

50 The *Red Lion* in West Street was not a posting house like the *Crown* but the Reading coach, travelling through High Wycombe, Marlow and Henley, stopped here every Wednesday, Thursday and Saturday.

51 Other inns had a rôle as a base for carriers' carts. In the 1840s, Richard Robinson's wagon set out from the *Greyhound*, Spittal Street, on Mondays and Thursdays, bound for London via Maidenhead.

An Act for repairing, widening, turning, and altering, the Road leading from *Reading*, in the County of *Berks*, through *Henley*, in the County of *Oxford*, and *Great Marlow*, *Chipping Wycombe*, *Agmondesham*, and *Cheynes*, in the County of *Bucks*, and *Rickmansworth*, *Watford*, and *Saint Albans*, to *Hatfield*, in the County of *Hertford*; and also the Road leading out of the said Road, at *Marlow*, over *Great Marlow Bridge*, through *Bysham*, to or near the Thirty Mile Stone, in the Turnpike Road leading from *Maidenhead* to *Reading*.

WHEREAS the High Road leading from the Town of Reading, in the County of Berks, over Caversham Bridge, by the South Side of Lord Cadogan's Park, through Play-hatch, and to and through the Town of Henley upon Thames, in the County of Oxford, and by Greenland Farm, Mill End, and Medmenham, and to and through the Town of Great Marlow, in the County of Bucks, and by Handy Crofs, and to and through the Town of Chipping Wycombe, and over Wycombe Heath, through Wilden Lane, and to and through the Town of Agmondesham,

6 C 2

Preamble.

52 Road transport in the 18th century was promoted by turnpike trusts, committees of local gentry and businessmen who were empowered by a local act of Parliament to charge tolls on certain roads and to apply the money to road improvement. The Hatfield to Reading road was turnpiked in 1768 and passed through Amersham, High Wycombe, Marlow and Henley-on-Thames.

53 Jeffery's Map of 1770 shows the site of the turnpike house at the junction of the roads to Wycombe and to Little Marlow. At this point the road is marked as unfenced where it passed through Marlow's unenclosed common fields.

54 This obelisk was erected at the head of the High Street by the turnpike trustees in 1822. It gives the distance to Hatfield as 36 miles and that to Reading as 15 miles.

55 The 1768 Act provided for a branch of the Hatfield to Reading road crossing the Thames on the old wooden bridge, passing through Bisham, and joining the Bath Road at the 30th milestone. This cast-iron milepost, perhaps dating from the 1820s, stands on the west side of the road near Bisham church.

56 The road from Marlow to Stokenchurc was turnpiked in 1791, providing an improve route to the great road from London to Oxforc The turnpike road left Marlow via Dea Street, the poorer part of the town, whic was nicknamed the City. Here were th beerhouses called the *Bank of England*, th *Mint* and the *Royal Exchange*.

57 Milestones survive on most Bucking hamshire turnpike roads. Stones like this on at Lane End can still be seen along the lengt of the Marlow to Stokenchurch turnpike.

58 The opening of the Great Western Railway in 1838 killed the coaching trade overnight. Coaches and carriers' carts now plied between Marlow and the nearest station at Maidenhead. Towns like Marlow, which were bypassed by the railways, risked becoming commercial backwaters. The railway did not reach Marlow until 1873 when a short branch from Bourne End, on the Great Western line from Maidenhead to High Wycombe, was completed. This picture shows Marlow station soon after its opening.

59 The branch railway greatly enhanced Marlow's position as a riverside resort and as a fashionable place from which to travel to work in London.

60 When the line from Bourne End to High Wycombe was closed in 1970, the Marlow branch was retained as it still carried considerable commuter traffic.

61 The railway reduced the work available to wheelwrights and carriage builders like Warner and Drye. Their premises on the High Street are shown here.

62 Warner and Drye adapted also to the coming of the motor car, which made Marlow increasingly accessible to the tourist.

63 Marlow's rambling medieval church of All Saints', which features on early prints of the town, was urgently in need of repair by the 1830s. The building of the new pound lock in 1777 had raised the level of the river and the church was regularly flooded.

64 Inside, the old church was fitted up with a fine canopied pulpit and box pews. The wooden framing of the pews was said to be stained by flood water up to 17 ins. above the floor level.

65 The decision was taken not to repair but to rebuild the church. The style chosen was perpendicular gothic, popular in the early 19th century, but the rectangular shape and the lack of chancel was more typical of the previous century. The structure was of yellow brick with stone dressings. It was completed in 1835.

66 Inside the new church, a potentially light and airy preaching room was cluttered with box pews and further seating on galleries supported on iron columns. The arrangement, however, did provide seating for 1,200 people.

67 The *Swan*, which stood on the Causeway near to the church, was demolished in 1865 to make way for a new vicarage.

68 The church looked handsome enough from the outside with its finely detailed spire and low pitched roof partially hidden behind a parapet. In this early photograph it is shown after the building of the vicarage to the north-east side in 1865 but before a chancel was added to the church in 1875.

69 The interior of the church was transformed by the addition of a chancel, by the removal of the galleries in 1882 and by the installation of arcading supporting a more steeply pitched roof.

0 Today the church has an odd look with its brick nave, flint chancel and a mixture of window styles where some but not all of the original perpendicular windows have been replaced by more fashionable decorated windows.

1 Extra churches were built in many growing towns in the Victorian period. Holy Trinity church, built in Gun Lane in 1852, provided the poor but growing area in the north of the town with seats for 200 worshippers. It was designed by the celebrated Buckinghamshire architect, Gilbert Scott.

Trinity Church Marlow

72 The Independent Chapel, originally built in 1726, was also in need of repair in the 1830s. Again it was decided to rebuild and the present chapel with brick pilasters and stone detailing was opened in 1840. After further changes in 1863 it provided 500 sittings.

73 The Wesleyan Chapel in Spittal Street was rebuilt in 1900 and could seat 350 people.

4 The Baptist Chapel in Glade Road was built in 1885 with ace for 250 people. The façade was rebuilt in 1932.

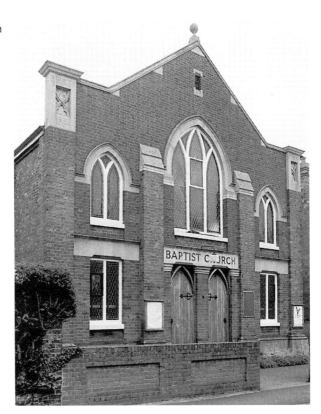

75 The Roman Catholic church on St Peter's Street is so near to the old Parsonage and its gothic architecture so authentic that it is difficult to believe that it was built as recently as 1846. The architect was Pugin and the cost was borne by Charles Scott-Murray, of Danesfield in Medmenham, who had recently converted to Catholicism.

76 A school, also designed by Pugin, was built to the south of the Roman Catholic church, and included this fine house for the schoolmaster.

77 The lord of the manor had the right to appoint a rector or parson and to receive the tithes (a tenth of a farmer's crop given to the church). In 1494, these rights were given to the Abbot of Tewkesbury who leased the parsonage and tithes and appointed a vicar on a lower salary to care for Marlow's spiritual needs. The parsonage in St Peter's Street has ever since been in lay hands, but the tenants continued to collect the tithes until 1843.

78 Marlow has a variety of grand houses built by families whose wealth came from outside the town. The Claytons, who purchased Harleyford in 1735 and built this house in 1755, owed their fortune to Sir Robert Clayton (1629-1707), a banker and financier who was Lord Mayor of London in 1679.

79 Court Garden was built about 1758 for Dr. William Battie (1704-1776), a successful physician and proprietor of a large private lunatic asylum in London. Battie's daughter, Anne, sold the house to another London surgeon, Richard Davenport, whose successors leased the house to a variety of tenants.

80 Dr. Battie was an architectural enthusiast and is said to have
designed Court Garden himself. It is claimed that he forgot to
include a staircase and that the basement rooms were often
under water.

81 In 1926, Court Garden was bought for the town by public
subscription. The trustees rented rooms to Marlow Urban District
Council which did not take over the house until 1955. The Council
remained there until local government re-organisation in 1974.

2 Marlow Place was built
around 1720 by John Wallop
(1690-1762), 1st Earl of
Portsmouth, a popular figure at
the Hanoverian court. He
inherited land in Marlow via his
mother Alicia, one of the
daughters of William Borlase.
She was still living at Marlow
Place in 1741.

83 Marlow Place was bought by the Claytons of Harleyford and sold on, with much of their property in the town, to Thomas Williams of Temple about 1790. In the 1860s, the Williams family let the house to Thomas Matthews who ran a boarding school there.

84 Cromwell House, on the right of this picture behind the cropped trees, appears to be of mid-18th-century date. It was the home of John Ellison, citizen of London, who died in 1743, according to a gravestone formerly within the old church. The Ellisons retained the house until about 1850. It has been more recently Marlow's post office.

85 A famous resident of Cromwell House was the engineer, Edwin Clark (1814-1894). Although he was not related to William Tierney Clark, designer of Marlow Bridge, he too built bridges and is best known as the resident engineer with Robert Stephenson on the box-girder Britannia Bridge over the Menai Strait in North Wales.

6 Thames Bank is another riverside retreat built about 1770 by Sarah Winford, whose daughter, Sarah, had married the wealthy Sambrooke Freeman of Fawley Court. This print shows that it had three storeys but Sarah Winford, who died in 1793, or her younger daughter Harriot, is said to have had the top storey removed, fearing that one of her numerous servants might accidentally set fire to the house.

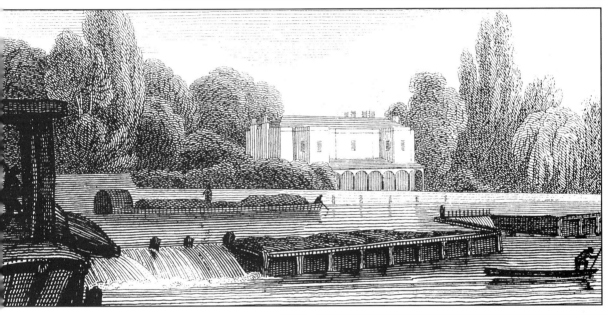

7 Thames Bank was bought in 1811 by Vice Admiral Sir James Nicoll Morris who had commanded H.M.S. *Colossus* at the battle of Trafalgar. His nephew Thomas Somers Cocks, a London banker, extended the grounds by purchasing a wharf and a beerhouse called the *Watermans Arms*, which stood at the end of St Peter's Street.

8 Now known as Thames Lawn, the house was owned from 1945 until his death in 1964 by the Birmingham property developer Jack Cotton. It was gutted by fire in 1992 and now awaits reconstruction.

89 Old Bridge House occupies the site of a group of old cottages, including the *Black Boy Inn*, which stood at the end of St Peter's Street. It was built about 1872 by another London banker named Hoare.

90 Remnantz is an early 18th-century house named after Stephen Remnant, son of a Woolwich ironfounder who supplied armaments to the government. This may explain why the house was leased to the Royal Military College in 1802. It has a lavish stable block, parallel with West Street, surmounted by a clock turret.

91 Western House has an elegant summer house built on to the corner of the garden wall fronting West Street. The initials CM and date 1699 on the rain-water heads suggest the house could have been built for Jonathan Hammond alias Cooper who is named in contemporary deeds. The Hammond family, who were gentleman farmers, continued to live there until the 1850s.

92 Gyldernscroft was an ancient farmstead belonging to the Langley family. Thomas Langley (1769-1801), author of the *History of Desborough Hundred*, bequeathed the house to his cousin, Lt. Col. Alexander Higginson, in whose family it descended until modern times.

93 This house on West Street is famous for being th residence in 1817 of the poet Shelley. Mary Shelle wrote in December 1817, 'This house is very damp, a the books in the library are mildewed'.

94 Until the 1832 Reform Act, Marlow was parliamentary borough electing two MPs. The Clayton of Harleyford could rely on their tenants in the town t support the family candidate for at least one of th seats. Sir William Clayton (1762-1834) sold much o his Marlow property in about 1790 to Thomas Williams so losing control of this pocket borough.

5 The owners of Bisham Abbey on the other side of the river also saw Marlow as their natural political base and the Hobby family of Bisham often held one of the seats.

6 Thomas Williams, proprietor of Temple Mills, bought up much of the Clayton property in Marlow in the late 18th century. He was MP for Marlow in 1790 and his family or their nominees continued to hold both Marlow seats until 1831.

97 The 1832 Reform Act intended that towns like Marlow should cease to be pocket boroughs. The boundary of the borough was extended to include Little Marlow, Medmenham and Bisham. Little changed, however, for the Williams family continued to dominate elections, the second seat often going to a relative and fellow Conservative.

8 The second Reform Act of 1867 reduced Marlow's representation to one member. The following year, the Liberals tried Edmund Hope Verney as candidate for the single seat but he was beaten by the brewer, Thomas Owen Wethered. Wethered represented Marlow for the Conservatives from 1868-1880.

9 The *Crown*, headquarters of the Conservative campaign, was attacked by rioters following the success of Thomas Price Williams at the election of 1880.

100 Wethered's Brewery was also the object of the rioters' wrath in 1880. The 1885 Redistribution of Seats Act finally deprived Marlow of separate representation, and the town became part of the Southern (Wycombe) Division of Buckinghamshire.

101 Petty sessions were held here at the Court, built in Trinity Road in 1869. A county police force had been set up in 1857 and police stations of this design can be found in many of Buckinghamshire's small towns.

102 Sir William Borlase, in founding a school in Marlow in 1624, was concerned as much with poverty as ignorance. He provided a building for the education of poor boys from Great and Little Marlow and Medmenham and an endowment for the more able to be apprenticed to a trade.

103 Borlase's intentions are made clear in the terms of establishing this Workhouse and House of Correction, where poor girls were to be taught the art of bone lace making and where rogues and vagabonds were to be detained. The building adjoined the free school.

104 Borlase's school remained a charity school until 1880 when re-organised as a fee-paying grammar school with scholarships available to children from the elementary schools of Great and Little Marlow and Medmenham.

105 Marlow was one of the first towns to have a National School, provided by the National Society for the Education of the Poor in the Principles of the Established Church. At first it was held in the house of the appointed schoolmaster but later the school was housed in a former Sunday School built here on the Causeway in 1851.

106 Marlow had no British School, that is one built for the children of non-conformists, nor did it establish a Board School under the 1870 Education Act. This boys' school, built in 1913 on what is now Wethered Road, replaced the National School building on the Causeway.

107 The Great Marlow Institute was founded in 1853 but moved to these premises in 1890. It had a library, newspaper, reading and recreation rooms. The County Library rented a room here in 1954 and bought the building following the closure of the Institute in 1957. It was reopened as a library in 1959.

108 Until the 1834 Poor Law Act, each parish was responsible for its own poor and larger parishes like Marlow had erected workhouses where the poor were required to work for their keep. The Workhouse, which still stands to the west of the Stokenchurch road, continued in use until the new Wycombe Union Workhouse at Saunderton was built in 1843.

109 The Oxford Lane Almshouses were endowed by John Brinkhurst in 1608 for the accommodation of six poor widows. They were demolished in 1969 and replaced by these flats. The Brinkhursts had owned both Temple Mills and Marlow Mills and a valuable part of the endowment was Brinkhurst's Wharf at the end of St Peter's Street.

110 A cottage hospital, paid for by public subscription, was opened in Cambridge Street in 1889. The Matron, Sister Cole, is seen standing outside.

111 Hospital Sunday was a popular means of raising money for the local hospital. Here a collector with a money-box on the end of a long pole receives donations from High Street proprietors who still lived over the shop in the 1920s.

112 The Cottage Hospital moved to these purpose-built premises in Glade Road in 1915.

113 Government of the town was entrusted in 1896 to Marlow Urban District Council. Members of the Council are shown here cutting the first sod of the sewage scheme in 1928.

114 After the First World War, the national government required local authorities to assess local housing needs. Money was given to local authorities to clear and replace unsanitary dwellings such as these cottages in Dean Street.

115 Marlow's population had increased from 3,236 in 1801 to 5,645 in 1901. These early 19th-century cottages in Cambridge Road would have been rented by skilled workmen.

116 Marlow's population growth accelerated after 190[and houses like these in Crov Road would be accessible those who could afford building society mortgage.

117 Marlow's growth enabled the local building firm of Y.J. Lovell to prosper. The firm's yard and joinery shops wer on the High Street.

118 The size of Y.J. Lovell's workforce can be judged from the numbers taking part in the 1924 works outing.

119 Marlow U.D.C. built these council houses on Seymour Court Road about 1938. They were designed to meet government standards of room size and amenities.

120 Council house building continued after the Second World War. These Georgian-style houses with sash windows were built in Dean Street about 1955.

121 In the 1930s, some Londoners who could leave the city in their cars built weekend homes on plots of land bought cheaply from local farmers. During the war, families escaping from the bombing occupied the houses continually and with increasing property values since the war, most have been replaced by larger brick-built houses. These shacks remained at Marlow Bottom in 1963.

122 Marlow Town Hall was built in 1807 at the expense of Thomas Williams of Temple House. It did little to enhance Marlow's position as a market town, for a directory of 1830 described the market as 'very trifling, if of any importance to the trade of this place'.

123 The arches under the Town Hall were meant to provide space for a covered market, but the town's fire brigade used part of the space for the horse-drawn fire engine. The brigade is shown outside the Town Hall in 1909.

124 John and Thomas Rolls were wharfingers and coal and timber merchants at Marlow Wharf. This 1836 catalogue of sale shows that they used the Market Square for their auctions.

GREAT MARLOW,

BUCKS.

TO BE

SOLD BY AUCTION,

BY

Messrs. Rolls,

On Saturday, February 20, 1836,

IN THE MARKET PLACE,

AT TWELVE O'CLOCK PRECISELY,

Under distress for Rates, under the Great Marlow Church Act of Parliament.

CATALOGUE.

LOT		CWT.	QR.	lb.
1	One bale of coarse rags, marked	6	0	6
2	Ditto, ditto - - - - -	5	2	23
3	Ditto, ditto - - - - -	5	3	6
4	Ditto, ditto - - - - -	5	1	0
5	Ditto, ditto - - - - -	4	3	15
6	Ditto, ditto - - - - -	5	2	14
7	Set of brass mounted chaise harness			
8	Twelve olive round frocks			
9	Eight pair of fustian trowsers			
10	A useful bay mare			
11	A ditto grey gelding			

May be Viewed the Morning of Sale, and Catalogues had of the Auctioneers, Marlow.

125 With the coming of the railway, the firm, now Rolls & Lawrence, ran a cattle market near the railway station.

MARLOW CATTLE MARKET.

SCALE OF CHARGES.

FAT AND STORE BEASTS AND COWS.

	AT PER HEAD.
	£ s. d.
On £25 and under	0 5 0
Above £25 and under £40..	0 7 6
Above £40	0 10 0
On Store Stock under £8 in value (if offered more than two in a lot)	0 3 6

CALVES.

On 20/- and under	0 1 0
On 40/-	0 1 6
On 50/-	0 2 0
On 120/-	0 2 6
Above 120/-	0 3 6

SHEEP AND LAMBS.

On Sheep and Lambs	0 1 0
On Store Sheep and Lambs (if 20 or more be sold in one lot)	0 0 9

PIGS.

On 20/- and under	0 0 6
On 20/- and under 30/-	0 0 9
On all above 30/- 2½ per cent.	
Sows and Hogs under £5 each, if sold singly	0 2 6

HORSES.

A Commission of £5 per cent. (in no case less than 5/-)	
On Horses bought in, over £10 reserve	0 5 0
" " under "	0 2 6

On all Unsold Lots a Charge of 1/- per Lot.

ROLLS & LAWRENCE,
Auctioneers, Land Agents, &c.,
GREAT MARLOW.

126 Prominent among the butchers in the town was William Robert Clark, whose shop is shown here on the High Street.

127 W.H. Outlaw's butcher's shop was in the Market Square. These animals were prize-winners at the Christmas Fat Stock show about 1914.

28 From a very early date, Marlow's river link with London had led local families to apprentice sons to London merchants and wealthy Londoners to set up house here. The High Street therefore has an unusual number of fine houses for a town of Marlow's size.

129 The influx of wealthy families continued as the railway replaced the river as the communication with London. The tradesmen on the High Street benefited greatly from the well-to-do families requiring provisions and the increasing numbers of visitors.

130 Marlow had its own department store on the west side of the High Street, run by the Morgan family who lived at the
Parsonage in St Peter's Street. The shop had three entrances, for furniture and carpets, for haberdashery and for men's and
boys' clothing, whilst ladies' dresses and children's clothes were upstairs.

131   The multiple stores began to move into the High Street about 1900. Freeman, Hardy & Willis were
selling modestly-priced footwear on the east side of High Street in the 1920s.

132 No.12 High Street was taken over by the International Tea Company which came to Marlow in the 1890s. The photograph was taken in 1943.

133 At no.16 High Street, Boots took over an old established chemist's shop in the 1930s.

34 The façades on High Street date mostly from the late 18th and early 19th century. The houses with Venetian windows, ccupied by antique dealers in this photograph of 1942, have been demolished, but the building on the left with bow indows has been incorporated into a new shopping development.

606 MARLOW. — *West Street.* — LL.

135 Several gentry families had their houses in West Street. The prosperity of the street is shown in this turn-of-the-century postcard.

136 This large 17th-century house on the north side of West Street has unusual finials on each gable. They are made of terracotta. The house has been divided into shops including in 1943, those of Fred Todd, tailor, Mrs. East, china-dealer and Christopher East, cobbler.

37 Also prominent on West Street were the premises of Batting & Sons, high class ironmongers and makers of agricultural machinery, both at Maidenhead and Marlow.

138 A root drilling machine made by Battings of Marlow is still in use at Widmere Farm.

139 Marlow was in the medieval period sometimes called 'Chepping Marlow' denoting a market, but no market charter has survived. Marlow also had two fairs, one in May and one in October. The May fair had ceased by the 19th century but the cattle fair continued to be held each October. Here the fair is shown in West Street, *c*.1900.

140 With the provision of a cattle market near the railway station, the streets were left free for the pleasure aspects of the fair, shown here at the lower end of High Street. In 1903, an order was made prohibiting the holding of the fair in the street.

41 The changing rôle of Marlow is well illustrated by this photograph of a well-dressed family at their leisure with a boat house on the former coal wharf to the west of the suspension bridge.

142 Turn of the century photographs of Marlow show increasing numbers of pleasure craft rather than commercial barges approaching Marlow Lock.

143 (*top left*) Marlow became a fashionable resort for the angling fraternity. Even on this early print, dating from about 1810, two cadets are shown fishing while two others, also with fishing rods, are seen talking to their lady friends, with the *Compleat Angler* in the background.

144 (*left*) Marlow became a fashionable resort for the angling fraternity. The *Compleat Angler* features on many views and is seen here with a pleasure boat moored nearby.

145 (*above*) The *Compleat Angler* is now a luxury Thames-side hotel. Even by the 1950s, it had been greatly enlarged and improved.

146 Another fashionable lodging for the anglers was the *Fisherman's Retreat* in St Peter's Street. It was formerly called the *Barge Pole*.

147 Jerome K. Jerome, author of *Three Men in a Boat*, used to stay at the *Fisherman's Retreat*. The building has now been enlarged and converted into several houses.

148 The *George and Dragon*, a fine inn on the Causeway, also began to market its accommodation to the anglers.

149 The gentry of Marlow sponsored the Marlow Races, depicted here in 1833. The course was on the meadowland between Marlow Mills and the bend in the river.

MARLOW RACES, 1839,

Will take place on WEDNESDAY and THURSDAY, 7th and 8th of AUGUST, over that delightful and well known Course, unrivalled for its beautiful situation and splendid scenery,---within Six Miles of the **GREAT WESTERN RAILWAY STATION**, from which Coaches and other Conveyances will run to and from.

FIRST DAY.

A SILVER CUP, the gift of LT. COL. SIR W. R. CLAYTON, BART. M. P. value 20 Guineas, added to a Sweepstakes of 5 Sovereigns each, for Horses of all ages. Twice round, heats. To start at the Winning Stand; three yrs. old, 7st. 4lb. four yrs. 8st. 8lb. five yrs. 9st. six and aged, 9st. 4lb. Mares and Geldings allowed 3lb. Winner to be sold for 100 Sovereigns, if demanded, &c. Six Subscribers or no Race. Entrance 10s. each, to go to the Fund.

LADIES PURSE of 20 Sovereigns, added to a Sweepstakes of 5 Sovereigns each. Six Subscribers or no Race. Twice round, heats. To start at the Winning Stand; three yrs. old, 7st. 4lb. four yrs. 8st. 8lb. five yrs. 9st. six and aged, 9st. 4lb. Mares and Geldings allowed 3lb. The Winner to be sold for 100 Sovereigns, if demanded, &c. Entrance 10s. each, to go to the Fund.

SWEEPSTAKES of 5 Sovereigns each, with a Purse added, for Galloways not higher than 14 hands. Six Subscribers or no Race. Twice round, heats. To start at the Winning Stand; 13 hands high to carry 8st. 2lb. 13½ hands, 8st. 10lb. 14 hands, 9st. 2lb. Entrance 10s. each, to go to the Fund.

SECOND DAY.

A PLATE, of 20 Sovereigns, added to a Sweepstakes of 5 Sovereigns each. Horses which won the First Day to carry 7lb. extra. Twice round, heats. To start at the Winning Stand. Six Subscribers or no Race. Three yrs. old, 7st. 4lb. four yrs. 8st. 8lb. five yrs. 9st. six and aged, 9st. 6lb. Mares and Geldings to be allowed 3lb. Winner to be sold for 100 Sovereigns, if demanded, &c. Entrance 10s. each, to go to the Fund.

SWEEPSTAKES of 5 Sovereigns each, for Galloways, with a Purse added. To carry the same weights as for the previous Stakes for Galloways. Winner of the First Day's Galloways Stakes to carry 5lb. extra. Six Subscribers or no Race. Twice round, heats. To start at the Winning Stand. Entrance 10s. each, to go to the Fund.

HURDLE RACE, of 3 Sovereigns each, with a Purse added. Once round, heats. To start from Ditch-in. Four sets of Hurdles. Horses to carry 11st. 4lb. each. If 4 or more Horses run, the owner of the second Horse to receive back his Stake. The Winner to be sold for 70 Sovereigns, if demanded, &c. Entrance 1 Sovereign each, to go to the Fund.

If any of the Stakes are walked over for, the public money will not be added. Winners of each Race to pay 2 Sovereigns to the Racing Fund. Winners at these Races last year to carry 5lb. extra.

Horses for the First Day's Races to be entered at the Crown Inn, between the hours of Six and Eight o'clock on Tuesday Evening, August 6th.—Double Entrance to be paid after that time. Horses for the Second Day's Races to be entered between the hours of Eight and Half-past Ten o'clock, on Thursday Morning, August 8th.—No Entrance will be taken after that time.

Lt. Col. Sir W. R. CLAYTON, Bart. M. P. } STEWARDS.
GEORGE SIMON HARCOURT, Esq. M. P. }

Matches or Heats, to be run, on permission being first obtained of the Stewards; and all disputes to be decided by them, and their decision to be final. All Dogs seen on the Course will be destroyed; and persons found damaging the Corn will be rigidly Prosecuted.

RIDERS to bring their Weights, and ride in proper Caps and Jackets. COLOURS to be named at Entrance, or 1 Sovereign penalty for neglecting so to do. Any attempt at unfair carrying of Weight, or Riding, or Dismounting until ordered by the Stewards, disqualifies from winning, or starting again. Half an Hour between each Heat, and no delay after the second Bell.—To start each Day precisely at One o'clock.

Application for Booth Standings to be made at the CROWN INN, on Saturday, August 3rd, by Nine o'clock. No Gambling Devices will be allowed on the Course. No Person to ride within the Lines, except the Riders for the Day's Racing, and the Officers of the Course, nor near the Horses when running.

** Subscription Books for next Year's Races will be opened each Day at the Winning Stand.

G. CANNON, PRINTER, MARLOW.

150 The opening of the railway line to Maidenhead in 1838 greatly increased the numbers attending the Marlow Races.

MARLOW AND RIVER THAMES.

151 No fashionable Thames-side resort was complete without a regatta. The first Marlow Regatta appears to have been held in 1855 but the Great Marlow Amateur Rowing Club was not formed until 1871.

GREAT MARLOW
REGATTA,

1855.

Open to AMATEURS and WATERMEN residing between WARGRAVE and BRAY inclusive.

This REGATTA will take place on THURSDAY,

16th of AUGUST,

INSTEAD of on THURSDAY, the 9th instant,
AS PREVIOUSLY ADVERTISED,

AT GREAT MARLOW,

Under the Patronage of the Gentry in the Neighbourhood.
When the following PRIZES will be contended for:—

1st. A PURSE of Two Guineas.
A SCULLING RACE.
FOR WATERMEN ONLY. HEATS, IF MORE THAN THREE START.

2nd. The SILVER OARS.
A PAIR-OAR RACE.
FOR AMATEURS ONLY. HEATS, IF MORE THAN THREE START. ENTRANCE-MONEY FIVE SHILLINGS.

3rd. A PURSE of Seven Guineas,
And One Guinea for the Second Boat.
A FOUR-OAR RACE.
FOR WATERMEN ONLY. HEATS, IF MORE THAN THREE START. THREE TO START, OR NO SECOND PRIZE WILL BE GIVEN.

4th. The SILVER SCULLS.
A SCULLING RACE.
FOR AMATEURS ONLY. HEATS, IF MORE THAN THREE START. ENTRANCE-MONEY HALF-A-CROWN.

5th. A PURSE of Three Guineas,
And Ten Shillings and Sixpence for the Second Punt.
A DOUBLE PUNT RACE.
THREE TO START, OR NO SECOND PRIZE WILL BE GIVEN.

6th. The CUP. A Four-Oar Race.
FOR AMATEURS ONLY. HEATS, IF MORE THAN THREE START. ENTRANCE-MONEY FIVE SHILLINGS.

7th. A PURSE of Four Guineas,
And One Guinea for the Second Boat.
A PAIR-OAR RACE.
FOR WATERMEN ONLY. HEATS, IF MORE THAN THREE START. THREE TO START, OR NO SECOND PRIZE WILL BE GIVEN.

8th. A Purse of One Guinea,
And Ten Shillings and Sixpence for the Second Punt.
A PUNT RACE.
THREE TO START, OR NO PRIZE WILL BE GIVEN TO THE SECOND PUNT.

All, who are desirous of entering Boats for the above PRIZES, will be required to give in their Names, and Colours, to the Committee, at the COMPLETE ANGLERS, any time between this and Twelve o'Clock on Wednesday, the 15th of August.
THE FIRST RACE WILL COMMENCE AT TWELVE O'CLOCK PRECISELY.
AN EXCELLENT BAND WILL ATTEND.
∵ SUBSCRIPTIONS will be received by W. L. WARD, Esq., Mr. T. ROSEWELL, Mr. JOSIAH CLARK, and Mr. G. CANNON, Library.

STEWARDS.
Major-Genl. Sir WILLIAM ROBERT CLAYTON, Bart.,
Sir GILBERT EAST GILBERT-EAST, Bart.,
Lt. Colonel BROWNLOW KNOX, M.P.,
B. ATKINSON, Esq.,
L. W. WETHERED, Esq.,
J. S. WILKINSON, Esq.

TREASURER.
W. L. WARD, Esq.

T. O. WETHERED, Secretary.

G. CANNON, PRINTER, MARLOW.

152 This poster advertising the first Marlow Regatta in 1855 shows that the event enjoyed the full support of the local gentry.

153 Shaw's boathouse, seen here by the bridge, was rebuilt about 1900. It has now been replaced by flats named Tierney Court after the bridge architect, William Tierney Clark.

154 The weekend of Marlow Regatta followed on from Ascot. Many visitors to the races moved on to Marlow. Here fashionable people hire punts from Shaw's boathouse by the bridge.

Bibliography

Butler, B.H., 'The Marlow tithes', *Records of Buckinghamshire* Vol.31, pp.1-12 1989

Cairns, A.J., *The book of Marlow* 1976

Cocks, A.H., 'Mr. Weller's drawings and prints', *Records of Buckinghamshire* Vol.10, pp.379-89 1915

Cocks, A.H., 'The parish Church of All Saints', Great Marlow', *Records of Buckinghamshire*, Vol.6, pp.326-40 1867

Colmer, F., 'Memorials of Marlow', Cuttings from the *Bucks Free Press*, 1932-33

Colvin, H.M., 'The architectural history of Marlow and its neighbourhood', *Records of Buckinghamshire*, Vol.15, pp.5-19 1947

Davies, R. & Grant, M.D., *Forgotten Railways: Chilterns and Cotswolds* 1975

Davis, R. W., *Political change and continuity 1760-1885: a Buckinghamshire study* 1972

Defoe, D., *A tour thro' the whole island of Great Britain* 3 vols., 1724-27 (Everyman edition, 2 vols., 1962)

Hepple, L.W. & Doggett, A.M., *The Chilterns* 1992

Karau, P. & Turner, C., *The Marlow branch* 1987

Langley, T., *The history and antiquities of the Hundred of Desborough* 1797

Lipscomb, G., *The history and antiquities of the County of Buckingham* 4 vols. 1847

'Marten', *Great Marlow: Parish and People in the 19th century* 1991

Morris, J. (Ed.), *Domesday Book: Buckinghamshire* 1978

Page, W. (Ed.), *Victoria History of the County of Buckingham* 4 vols. 1905-27

Plaisted, A. H., *The Romance of a Chiltern Village* 1958

Reed, M., *A History of Buckinghamshire* 1993

Reed, M., *The Buckinghamshire Landscape* 1979

Sheahan, J.J., *History and Topography of Buckinghamshire* 1862

Wilson, D.G., *The Making of the Middle Thames* 1977